T0334354

Cambridge Elements

Elements in Intercultural Communication
edited by
Will Baker
University of Southampton
Troy McConachy
University of New South Wales
Sonia Morán Panero
University of Southampton

ETHICAL GLOBAL CITIZENSHIP EDUCATION

Emiliano Bosio
Toyo University, Japan

CAMBRIDGE
UNIVERSITY PRESS

Shaftesbury Road, Cambridge CB2 8EA, United Kingdom

One Liberty Plaza, 20th Floor, New York, NY 10006, USA

477 Williamstown Road, Port Melbourne, VIC 3207, Australia

314–321, 3rd Floor, Plot 3, Splendor Forum, Jasola District Centre,
New Delhi – 110025, India

103 Penang Road, #05–06/07, Visioncrest Commercial, Singapore 238467

Cambridge University Press is part of Cambridge University Press & Assessment,
a department of the University of Cambridge.

We share the University's mission to contribute to society through the pursuit of
education, learning and research at the highest international levels of excellence.

www.cambridge.org
Information on this title: www.cambridge.org/9781009565219

DOI: 10.1017/9781009326742

First published 2024

A catalogue record for this publication is available from the British Library.

ISBN 978-1-009-56521-9 Hardback
ISBN 978-1-009-32675-9 Paperback
ISSN 2752-5589 (online)
ISSN 2752-5570 (print)

Ethical Global Citizenship Education

Elements in Intercultural Communication

DOI: 10.1017/9781009326742
First published online: November 2024

Emiliano Bosio
Toyo University, Japan

Author for correspondence: Emiliano Bosio, bosio@toyo.jp

Abstract: Global citizenship education (GCE) plays a central role within UNESCO's education sector, focusing on cultivating the values and knowledge essential for students to evolve into well-informed and responsible global citizens. This Element conceptualises an ethical GCE framework grounded in critical, cosmopolitan, humanistic, value-creating, and transformative principles. Guided by those principles, ethical GCE goes beyond the banking model of education by emphasising a global ethic. Ethical GCE is inclusive, ethically reflective, and socially responsible. It extends beyond imparting knowledge and employable skills, important as they are, focusing on holistic and sustainable development. With further theoretical development and implementation strategies, the ethical GCE framework holds promise for future research and evaluation of the intricate teaching and learning processes within global citizenship, particularly from a values-based perspective.

This Element also has a video abstract: www.cambridge.org/EIIC_Bosio

Keywords: global citizenship education, UNESCO, ethics, critical pedagogy, social justice, decolonialism

ISBNs: 9781009565219 (HB), 9781009326759 (PB), 9781009326742 (OC)
ISSNs: 2752-5589 (online), 2752-5570 (print)

Contents

1 Ethical Global Citizenship Education   1

2 Critical Principles of Ethical GCE   7

3 Cosmopolitan Principles of Ethical GCE   20

4 Humanistic Principles of Ethical GCE   25

5 Value-Creating Principles of Ethical GCE   28

6 Transformative Principles of Ethical GCE   34

7 Envisioning an Ethical GCE Reinforced by Value-Pluralism   39

References   54

1 Ethical Global Citizenship Education

1.1 Introduction

Globalisation has expanded the scope of citizenship education beyond traditional national boundaries. This shift demands renewed dedication from educators[1] worldwide to cultivate critical thinkers capable of navigating the complexities of contemporary societies (Bosio & Guajardo, 2024a; Bosio & Gregorutti, 2023a, 2023b, 2023c; Bosio, Torres, & Gaudelli, 2023; Bosio et al., 2023; Giroux & Bosio, 2021).

In this context, over the past decade, there has been increasing interest in global citizenship education (GCE). Global citizenship education plays a central role within UNESCO's education sector, focusing on cultivating the values and knowledge essential for students to evolve into well-informed and responsible global citizens[2] (Bosio, 2021a, 2021b). There has been considerable discussion of the ways in which GCE should develop in academia, with a range of theoretical positions being discussed in the literature. These positions span from critical, including decolonial and postcolonial (Pashby et al., 2020; Stein, 2015; Stein & Andreotti, 2021; Swanson & Pashby, 2016; Tarozzi & Torres, 2016) to humanistic (Guajardo, 2021) and value-creating (Sharma, 2018, 2020), from cosmopolitan (Appiah, 2006; Archibugi, 2002, 2008) to transformative (Bamber et al., 2017). UNESCO's (2015) definition of GCE is one of the most frequently employed. Global citizenship education is concerned with fostering 'the knowledge, skills, values and attitudes that learners need to be able to contribute to a more inclusive, just and peaceful world' (p. 15).

Ethical GCE, as conceptualised in this Element, is grounded in the values and knowledge of Paulo Freire's critical pedagogy and social justice (Freire, 1973, 1983, 2000), Andreotti's (2006, 2011) critical and decolonial perspectives as well as in cosmopolitan, humanistic, value-creating, transformative, and ethical principles of global citizenship as discussed by Pashby (2011), Pashby and Andreotti (2016), Stein (2018), Swanson and Gamal (2021), Torres and Tarozzi (2016), Oxley and Morris (2013), Sharma (2018, 2020), and others (Bosio, 2024; Bosio & Guajardo, 2024b; Bosio & Waghid, 2023a, 2023b; Giroux & Bosio, 2021;

---

[1] Throughout this Element, the terms educators, teachers, and academics will be used interchangeably. However, I acknowledge a distinction between simply imparting a 'list of facts' to students and assisting them in cultivating 'ethical values and knowledge' (e.g., critical consciousness, awareness of both environmental and social injustices). My understanding of the terms educators, teachers, and academics aligns with the latter, specifically aiming to foster a profound appreciation in students and inspire the type of learning that nurtures enduring values (e.g., appreciation for justice, compassion, responsibility, care, and creativity) that will last throughout their lives.

[2] In this Element, the term global citizen will denote individuals who have developed substantial critical awareness of both local and global issues impacting our planet (e.g., equity, diversity, climate change, human rights, women's rights) and actively engage in tangible actions for the common good. For more details, see Bosio and Schattle (2021a, 2021b).

McLaren & Bosio, 2022; Veugelers & Bosio, 2021). Particularly, though not limited to, principles of critical consciousness, praxis, reflexive and intercultural dialogue, de- and post-colonialism, ecopedagogy, caring ethics, and empowering humanity (Bosio, 2023a, 2023b, 2023c, 2032d; Bosio & Olssen, 2023; Bosio & Torres, 2020a, 2020b; Bosio & Waghid, 2023a, 2023b; Noddings, 2005/2018; Tarozzi & Inguaggiato, 2018; Tarozzi & Mallon, 2019).

Guided by those core principles, ethical GCE seeks to go beyond the banking model of education[3] by emphasising a global ethic[4] entrenched in value-pluralism[5]. From this perspective, the broad objective of ethical GCE is to cultivate in all learners – not only white, rich and located in the Global North – a sense of responsibility and common values that can potentially guide individuals and societies in their interactions, enabling them to address glocal[6] challenges in a manner that promotes sustainability and generates value for our shared planet, for, as Berners-Lee (2021) puts it, there is no Planet B.

1.2 Dimensions of Ethical Global Citizenship Education

The term 'ethical' within ethical GCE directs attention to all facets of the teaching/learning environment and the student experience, encompassing five dimensions: critical, cosmopolitan, humanistic, value-creating, and transformative (Figure 1).

As illustrated in Figure 1, each dimension presents a series of principles or pathways for teaching/learning within ethical GCE. For instance, the critical dimension of ethical GCE aims to cultivate in learners an understanding of principles such as decolonialism, caring ethics, eco-critical perspectives, critical consciousness, praxis, critical reflection/action, and reflexive dialogue. From this perspective, ethical GCE empowers learners, at least potentially, to critically

---

[3] The term 'banking model of education' depicts students as containers into which educators deposit knowledge (Freire, 2000). Freire contended that this model perpetuates a deficiency in critical thinking and ownership of knowledge, ultimately reinforcing oppression. In contrast, Freire advocated for an understanding of knowledge as an outcome of a critical and creative process.

[4] The notion of a global ethic, as I discuss it in this Element, acknowledges the interdependence of the world and underscores the need for a universal moral foundation to tackle global issues such as environmental sustainability, human rights, social justice, and world peace (see also Bosio & Schattle, 2021a).

[5] The notion of a value-pluralism, as I frame it in this Element, posits that there are numerous forms of knowledge and values that may be appropriate and necessary for students to learn (e.g., social justice, equity, respect, and integrity). This viewpoint is in line with Webster (2023), who suggests that instead of students being indoctrinated by academics into a singular set of values, it might be more relevant to nurture their ability to critically evaluate a variety of principles and bodies of knowledge.

[6] In this Element, the term glocal blends global and local, emphasising their interconnectedness. It highlights how global forces impact local contexts and vice versa, shaping economics, culture, and social issues.

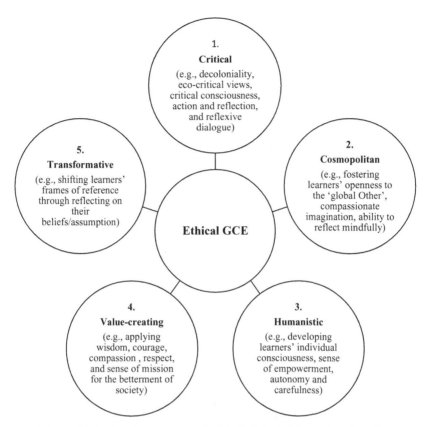

Figure 1 The five dimensions of ethical global citizenship education

examine their beliefs, positions, and identities within the complex framework of local and global structures. The cosmopolitan dimension of ethical GCE encourages learners to recognise the significance of compassion, the importance of balanced participation in global processes, and a genuine openness to understanding and engaging with the perspectives of both the global and local 'Others'. The humanistic dimension of ethical GCE supports the learner to develop global moral consciousness, autonomy, and carefulness while empowering their humanity. The value-creating dimension of ethical GCE nurtures learners' wisdom, courage, compassion, respect, and a sense of mission for the betterment of society. Lastly, the transformative dimension of ethical GCE assists learners in shifting their frames of reference by contemplating their beliefs and assumptions. This occurs as they are actively encouraged by their educators to engage in the intentional reconstruction of their worldview through actions that contribute to the common good (Bosio & Torres, 2019).

While the five dimensions of ethical GCE may overlap to some extent, they all converge to contribute to fostering the 'ethical global citizen' – an individual committed to critically understanding and respecting diverse perspectives, actively engaging in compassionate and reflective dialogue, and taking action to contribute to positive social and environmental change on a local and global scale.

The five dimensions are not intended to offer an exhaustive framework for ethical GCE, as the concept of ethical GCE is dynamic and continuously open to new refinements.

1.3 Distinctiveness of the Element

This element is ground-breaking in three different aspects. Firstly, it explores distinct ethical principles (e.g., critical consciousness, praxis, reflexive dialogue, decolonialism, eco-critical perspectives, caring ethics, and empowering humanity) within global citizenship, organised into a comprehensive ethical GCE framework. Secondly, it provides educators with a set of ideas to foster innovative pedagogical approaches at the classroom level, potentially bridging the divide between GCE theory and practical implementation. Thirdly, this Element shapes the conceptualisation of ethical GCE approaches to education on local and global citizenship in the era of increasing neoliberal globalisation and the definition of ethical values and knowledge within GCE.

The aim of this Element is to contribute to the redefinition of the role of contemporary ethical GCE pedagogy. This redefinition seeks to establish an ethical paradigm rooted in principles of reciprocity, mutuality, and social responsibility, as opposed to fostering market-driven, passive, and disengaged behaviours (Bosio & Torres, 2019; Freire, 1973).

Hence, the Element critically examines the concept of ethical GCE, exploring the fundamental values and knowledge that educators should cultivate in their students through this framework. Furthermore, it investigates whether ethical GCE holds the potential to represent a distinct paradigm for re-envisioning traditional forms of civic and citizenship education towards more ethical and sustainable perspectives. This involves embracing multicultural, critical, cosmopolitan, humanistic, transformative, and post/decolonial principles, as advocated by scholars such as Banks (2017, 2020, 2021), Freire and Macedo (1995), and Mignolo (2020a, 2020b).

The underlying questions that stretch through the entire Element are: How can we assist all learners in emancipating their lives and becoming ethical global citizens? What are some of the key values and knowledge that our students should be helped to develop through an ethical GCE?

To examine these and other related questions, the Element seeks to address a spectrum of pedagogical responses to contemporary societal challenges, such as racial discrimination, women's rights, and local and global inequities, engaging in reflexive analysis of the complexities, contestations, and agendas characterising the notion of ethical GCE amid the backdrop of growing globalisation.

1.4 Main Themes and Structure of the Element

This Element is divided into seven sections following this introduction, with a concluding section that summarises the Element's key arguments and perspectives. Each section explores various principles pertinent to ethical GCE, aiming to direct the reader's focus towards viewing ethical GCE not just as a marginal topic but as an essential component of teaching and learning.

Section 2 begins by laying out the critical principles of ethical GCE. It conceptualises ethical GCE as a Freirean critical pedagogy (Freire, 1973, 2000) centred on prioritising social justice and value-pluralism. By emphasising critical pedagogy, ethical GCE promotes social justice and extends beyond fostering students' basic interconnectedness and cultural awareness to situate discourse critically and reflectively within the globalised context. Based on its critical principles, ethical GCE encourages learners to analyse their preconceptions, positions, and identity in relation to the complexities of local/global structures. For instance, the principle of decoloniality invites learners to critically examine and challenge prevailing colonial narratives, encouraging a revaluation of historical perspectives. Ethics of care highlights the importance of nurturing students' emotions, such as empathy and compassion. Eco-critical values underscore the importance of ecological sustainability, promoting an awareness of the environmental impact of individual and collective actions. Critical consciousness urges learners to question assumptions, societal norms, and power structures. The integration of critical action and reflection emphasises the dynamic relationship between theory and practice, inspiring proactive engagement with global issues. Lastly, reflexive dialogue fosters open and inclusive conversations that promote understanding across diverse perspectives. These principles collectively form a robust and critical foundation for ethical GCE, fostering learners' multifaceted understanding of the interconnected nature of our global community towards sustainability.

Section 3 is concerned with the cosmopolitan principles of ethical GCE. It discusses ethical GCE as encompassing principles of openness to the glo-cal other, balanced participatory processes, and compassionate imagination. Embracing a profound openness to the glo-cal other, ethical GCE encourages learners to transcend geographical and cultural boundaries, cultivating a sense of interconnectedness with diverse perspectives worldwide. The emphasis on balanced participatory processes underscores the importance of inclusivity and collaboration. Ethical GCE strives to create learning environments where all voices are acknowledged and valued, promoting active engagement and shared responsibility in addressing local and global challenges. Herewith, a vital component of ethical GCE is compassionate imagination. This calls for a creative and empathetic understanding of the experiences and struggles of others. Informed by cosmopolitan principles, ethical GCE aims to transcend borders, both physical and conceptual, cultivating students' ability to reflect mindfully. This is a mindset that values the contributions of all individuals to the shared narrative of humanity.

Section 4 presents ethical GCE as adopting the humanistic principles of global moral consciousness, autonomy, and carefulness while empowering their humanity. This section underscores the importance of cultivating a deep-seated awareness of global moral issues, through which ethical GCE assists learners develop a sense of responsibility and ethical consideration for the well-being of humanity on a local and global scale. Autonomy is highlighted as one core principle, emphasising the significance of individuals having the freedom to think critically, make informed choices, and act in alignment with ethical values. Carefulness urges learners to approach global issues with sensitivity and thoughtfulness. This principle underscores the importance of considering the potential impacts of actions locally and globally, promoting a mindset of careful reflection and ethical consideration. By embracing these humanistic principles, ethical GCE seeks to not only impart knowledge and skills but also instil a profound sense of responsibility in learners.

Section 5 discusses ethical GCE as welcoming the value-creating principles of wisdom, courage, compassion, respect, and a sense of mission for the betterment of society. Wisdom encourages learners to cultivate a deep under-standing of glo-cal issues, integrating knowledge and insight to make informed decisions that positively impact society. Courage urges individuals to confront the challenges facing our super-complex societies with resilience and convic-tion. Compassion emphasises the importance of empathetic engagement with diverse perspectives and the struggles of others. The respect principle of ethical GCE involves appreciation of diverse cultures, beliefs, and experiences. A sense of mission for the betterment of society serves as a unifying force, inspiring learners to channel their knowledge and values towards positive social change. By embracing these value-creating principles, ethical GCE seeks to cultivate a commitment to living in a way that creates value for the betterment of society, aligning individual aspirations with the collective welfare of humanity.

Section 6 analyses the transformative principles of ethical GCE. Specifically, it focuses on the process of facilitating a shift in learners' frames of reference as they engage in introspection, challenging their existing beliefs and assumptions, and actively participate in the deliberate reconstruction of their worldview through action for the common good. By integrating transformative principles, ethical GCE is explored as a pedagogical platform aimed at supporting the learner as they transform their modes of being through holistic experiences ingrained in both the local and global context (e.g., holistic transformative).

Lastly, Section 7, envisions a GCE reinforced by value-pluralism. It serves as a summary for the entire Element. It proposes a vision for ethical GCE strengthened by value pluralism. Value pluralism embraces a range of values and knowledge that can be adopted and implemented to encourage ethical GCE teaching and learning pathways within educational institutions. These pathways can be ethical, critical, cosmopolitan, humanistic, value-creating, and transformative. Value-pluralistic ethical GCE transcends the mere 'dry technicality of skills' and maintains a central pedagogical focus on environmental sustainability, social justice, critical consciousness, caring ethics, ecology, and human empowerment. With a strong commitment to these pedagogical objectives, value-pluralistic ethical GCE offers the possibility of redirecting teaching and learning towards more holistic and ethically oriented goals. This includes developing learners into accountable, emancipated, creative, and empathetic global citizens within a democratic society.

2 Critical Principles of Ethical GCE

In this section, I examine the critical principles of ethical GCE: (a) decolonialism; (b) caring ethics; (c) eco-critical views; (d) critical consciousness; (e) praxis; (f) critical reflection; (g) critical action; and (h) reflexive dialogue.

Based on these critical principles, ethical GCE seeks to foster social justice in all learners, not just those who are white, rich, and located in the Global North. Ethical GCE goes beyond cultivating students' basic interconnectedness and cultural awareness. Thus, I situate ethical GCE critically and reflectively within the neoliberal globalised context, drawing on the work of critical and decolonial scholars including Andreotti (2006, 2011), Swanson and Pashby (2016), Tarozzi and Torres (2016), Giroux and Bosio (2021), and McLaren and Bosio (2022).

2.1 Decolonialism

With the dominance of neoliberalism, uneven globalisation is a prevailing reality, resulting in an unequal distribution of power between the Northern and Southern regions of the world. It is important to recognise that the issues at hand extend beyond poverty or development. They encompass broader concerns of injustice and inequality (Bosio & Olssen, 2023).

The decolonial stance on ethical GCE involves educators focusing on how knowledge is produced, fostering hyper-self-reflexivity, emphasising pedagogical dissensus to help learners navigate complexity and paradox, and striving to move ethical discussions beyond ethnocentrism and absolute relativism (Bosio, 2023).

Hence, ethical GCE necessitates educators to foster critical literacy among students. Critical literacy empowers learners to scrutinise their own identities, positions, and preconceived notions in the context of the intricate web of local and global issues (e.g., food insecurity, climate change, environmental disasters, pandemic, refugee rights, gender equality) (Bosio & Waghid, 2023a).

It is important to emphasise that critical literacy in ethical GCE is not about uncovering a singular, ultimate truth for students. Instead, it revolves around creating a teaching and learning environment in which students can honestly reflect upon their own ontological and epistemological assumptions while respecting the perspectives and beliefs of others (Bosio & Waghid, 2023b).

From a critical standpoint, I differentiate educators' ethical GCE approach from the 'soft' liberal perspective, advocating for decoloniality and embracing diversity over neutral universal subjectivities. Educators adopting such critical literacy approaches may function as cultural agents, facilitating negotiations between diverse viewpoints to prevent the perpetuation of harmful stereotypes for students. Critical and postcolonial theory underscores that discussions about neoliberalism, globalisation, and internationalisation may unintentionally reinforce inequalities within colonial relations (Stein & Andreotti, 2021).

This sort of value-orientation would suggest that conceptualising an ethical GCE means also to pay 'attention to the false universalism of globalisation and shows how contemporary social, political, economic, and cultural practices continue to be located within the processes of cultural domination through the imposition of imperial structures of power' (Rizvi, 2007, p. 256).

These viewpoints suggest that educators, through ethical GCE, endeavour to address injustice, exploitation, and inequality imposed on former colonies via (neo-)colonisation, with the intention to scrutinise 'the persistent "neo-colonial" relations within the "new" world order ... ' (Bhabha, 1994, p. 6). Educators employing this approach, ideally at least, 'attempt to shift the dominant ways in which the relations between Western and non-Western people and their worlds are viewed' (Young, 2003, p. 2).

2.2 Caring Ethics

Care ethics underscores the importance of cultivating empathy and compassion in students. These emotions enable them to see the world from the perspectives of others, fostering a heightened awareness and sensitivity to the needs of others.

From an ethical standpoint, I propose that ethical GCE helps students recognise the complexity of their relationships on global, national, and local levels, which give rise to various forms of inclusion and exclusion. Simply put, ethical GCE assists learners to understand that power and wealth are not only unevenly distributed within civilisations but also on a global scale (North/South divide).

In line with this perspective, ethical GCE educators incorporate critical principles that necessitate active engagement with current local and global issues to advance equality, justice, and peace. These principles encompass both political and social commitments (Veugelers & Bosio, 2021).

Ethical GCE, guided by critical principles, highlights the disparities stemming from globalisation and encourages critical examination of the international power structures perpetuating the North-South divide and global inequality. It stems from a strong moral stance against social injustice and seeks to forge bonds of solidarity among marginalised groups, motivating them to take direct action to bring about significant local and global changes; for instance, by seeking to transform the colonial mindset of international financial institutions.

According to this viewpoint, educators who embrace ethical GCE also have a responsibility to promote an 'ethics of care'. This involves, as highlighted by Noddings (2012), an academic discussion regarding the core components necessary to cultivate a caring relationship in teaching and learning. These components encompass pedagogical objectives such as fostering students' critical consciousness, encouraging reflective dialogue, and empowering humanity.

Respecting individuals and their rights is a fundamental aspect of ethical GCE. Human rights, particularly those related to women, as well as the core tenets of feminism as articulated in the influential writings of bell hooks (real name Gloria Jean Watkins), are integral to the perspective of an ethically engaged educational institution striving to cultivate critical consciousness (Bosio, 2023a; Bosio & Gregorutti, 2023a, 2023b).

Though bell hooks has sadly passed away, her important themes regarding sexual objectification, patriarchy, oppression, and stereotyping continue to resonate in feminist theory, as evident in her works such as *Talking Back: Thinking Black, Thinking Feminist* (Hooks, 1989) and *Feminist Theory from Margin to Centre* (Hooks, 1984). Ethical GCE is most effectively pursued within a social justice and human rights model, provided these goals are successfully achieved.

From this viewpoint, ethical GCE transcends mere cognitive learning and technocratic thinking solely focused on quantifiable outcomes. It aligns with the

UNESCO commission report *Learning: The Treasure Within*[7], which empha-sises the prominence of holistic education encompassing aspects like spiritual-ity, art, aesthetics, and ethics, all aimed at fostering a sense of peace and harmony among individuals and with the planet.

In an era where neoliberal concepts of self-directed learning, competitive individualism, and personalised modules have gained prominence, ethical GCE advocates for learning approaches that place a strong emphasis on collective ethics of knowledge.

2.3 Eco-critical Perspective

The eco-critical element of ethical GCE recognises the disparities between individual cultures and the prevailing cultures of humanity concerning their ecological orientations. It encompasses the capacity to challenge assumptions that underpin unjust suffering in society and environmental degradation.

It also involves the ability to scrutinise and analyse cultural and linguistic aspects, along with their associated beliefs and values, which have contributed to shaping human thought and, in turn, perpetuating injustice (Lupinacci & Happel-Parkins, 2016a, 2016b).

Ethical GCE educators prioritise values related to diversity and the eco-social structural correlations evident in language, culture, and education. They seek to play a crucial role in reshaping students' recognition and understanding of differences. For instance, in response to the lack of an English term that encapsulates humans' relationship with the nonhuman environment in a harmonious, respectful, and pragmatic way, Bosio (2021a) and Lupinacci (2017) introduce the term 'eco-tistical' to the conversation.

Weintraub et al. (2006, p. 55) attempt to fill the gap by replacing 'eco-' for 'ego-' to create an antonym for 'anthropocentric' (centred around humans) and 'egocentric' (centred around the self). This linguistic shift redirects the focus away from the self and towards a 'planetarian ethics'. Within this framework, ecocentrism characterises ecological consciousness, which Martusewicz and Edmondson (2005) describe as an 'eco-ethical consciousness' (p. 73). This perspective considers the repercussions of human decisions on both the envir-onment and society, recognising their intrinsic interconnectedness.

It is essential to recognise that in both Western and Eastern industrial cultures, humans have historically framed themselves as a species existing in isolation and superiority compared to all other beings on Earth, be they animate or inanimate. Therefore, framing discussions about ethical GCE within the context

---

[7] Full report available here: https://unesdoc.unesco.org/ark:/48223/pf0000109590

of the growing body of scholarship on eco-critical, eco-ethical, or eco-tistical values is significant (Bosio & Waghid, 2022b).

To capture the deeper ecological relationships extending beyond systems solely focused on human-human interactions, Abram (1999) introduces the concept of 'more-than-human'. This term is especially relevant to my discussion on ethical GCE as it encompasses all living entities, including rocks, soil, forests, rivers, animals, and plants. It emphasises interconnectedness that extends beyond humans alone. For instance, Bosio (2020) advocates for an eco-ethical approach to GCE pedagogy, emphasising the importance of fostering awareness regarding the interwoven relationships between humans and the environment. Bosio (2020) highlights the necessity of integrating education for social and ecological justice.

From this angle, through an ethical GCE conceptualised from an ecocritical perspective educators seek to encourage learners to examine the injustice created by humanity's perception that it is the supreme being on Earth.

Ethical GCE, grounded in eco-critical knowledge and values, has as one of its explicit purposes the disruption and reconstitution of Western industrial attitudes that influence and structure the patterns of education. It assists students in understanding the interrelationships of human beings, particularly the ways in which they relate to the ecosystem of which they are just one part.

2.4 Critical Consciousness

Ethical GCE extends beyond conventional paradigms of knowledge acquisition to embrace a more extensive pedagogical mission – namely, the cultivation of responsible and conscientious global citizens. At its core, ethical GCE strives to empower learners with the requisite knowledge, values, and perspectives essential for critical engagement with the complex global landscape, the redress of societal injustices, and the promotion of positive transformative change.

Critical consciousness in ethical GCE assumes a pivotal role, encouraging learners to scrutinise power dynamics, question established norms, and foster profound empathy for marginalised communities. The concept of critical consciousness, deeply rooted in the educational philosophy of Brazilian pedagogue Paulo Freire (Freire, 1973) is associated with a wide spectrum of pedagogical advantages. These encompass students' capacity for critical reflection, the exercise of political agency, the undertaking of critical action, heightened motivation, sustained engagement, resilience in the face of challenges, and active involvement in civic and political spheres (El-Amin et al., 2017).

While interpretations of critical consciousness vary (Bosio & Waghid, 2023a), in the context of this discussion on ethical GCE, it pertains to the acquisition of a comprehensive understanding of the world, taking into account an awareness of, and exposure to, political and social contradictions. It entails the cultivation of one's identity through a dialectical interplay between the local and global dimensions of existence. It involves the transmission of intangible values to students, including a profound sense of solidarity, a reverence for humanity, and the recognition that our planet represents the sole abode available to us.

The development of critical consciousness within the realm of ethical GCE necessitates a thoughtful recognition of disparities in power and social status, accompanied by a profound shift in perspective towards a firm commitment to the cause of social justice. An ethical GCE programme focused on fostering students' critical consciousness can be developed by drawing upon the insights of Argentinean sociologist Dussel (1977, 1996, 2019). In particular, Dussel's examination of Eurocentrism serves as a valuable foundation, wherein he highlights that Eurocentrism is frequently rationalised by the notion that Europe possesses distinctive traits (such as rationality) that warrant its superiority over other cultures. Dussel (1977, 1996, 2019) contends that this perspective places Europe at the core of a system whose overarching ideology justifies its global dominance and validates its colonialist pursuits.

Critical consciousness in ethical GCE entails a cognitive and emotional process, which, in turn, leads to collaborative problem-solving through participatory dialogue and the restoration of a more humane dimension to human–human and human–nature interactions. Notably, the perpetuation of inequality is often rooted in the inability of those most affected by discrimination to fully comprehend their social circumstances and disadvantages (Freire, 2004).

Within the framework of ethical GCE, critical consciousness development involves a deliberate examination of the pervasive disparities in privilege, power, and income. This process entails a fundamental shift in perspective towards a profound commitment to the cause of social justice. These disparities manifest themselves in various social relationships.

In the context of ethical GCE, the term 'conscientisation', employed by Freire (1973), denotes a complex process that encompasses both cognitive and emotional dimensions. It culminates in collaborative problem-solving through active and interactive communication, ultimately leading to the re-humanization of interpersonal relationships (Freire, 1973; Young, 2008).

One of the primary objectives of ethical GCE involves eliminating barriers to education that often stem from racial and social differences. Freire (1973) astutely observed that inequality persists because those most affected by it often struggle to fully grasp the extent of their social circumstances. In response, Freire proposed a cycle for the development of critical consciousness, consisting of:

- developing a sense of agency or empowerment
- gaining insight into the structures and mechanisms that perpetuate inequality through critical analysis
- committing to proactive action against oppressive circumstances through critical action (Freire, 1973).

From this perspective, the critical consciousness component of ethical GCE aims to reinforce individuals' dedication to combating systemic injustices. El-Amin et al. (2017) have noted that heightened critical awareness of the societal mechanisms of oppression can replace feelings of isolation and self-blame with a sense of involvement in a collective effort for social justice. For instance, a deeper understanding of racism may motivate Black students to actively pursue academic excellence and remain in school, challenging oppressive conditions.

To effectively incorporate critical consciousness into the pedagogy of ethical GCE, educators may thoughtfully integrate critical and social justice-oriented ideals into their instruction on both local and global citizenship. These ideals encompass a range of concepts, including (among others):

- democracy
- diversity
- equity
- participation
- human rights (Bosio & Waghid, 2022b).

The aim of ethical GCE is then to foster a morally upright, socially just, ecologically conscious, and economically sustainable human society. From an educational perspective, the focus shifts towards cultivating critical knowledge and values, in addition to imparting job-market skills, recognising that both elements are essential in preparing students to be responsible and ethical global citizens.

2.5 Praxis

In ethical GCE, critical consciousness development is not a linear process but rather cyclical. Students do not simply attain critical consciousness; it is a continuous journey. Praxis represents the ongoing process of critical consciousness development, wherein educators motivate students to participate in both reflection and action. Freire (1973, p. 51) defines praxis as 'critical reflection and action upon the world to transform it'. According to Freire (1973), individuals must take deliberate action to bring about a more just world; merely studying the external world is insufficient. Freire (1973, p. 51) suggests that 'human nature is revealed through deliberate, reflective, and meaningful engagement situated within dynamic historical and cultural contexts that both influence and set boundaries on such engagement'. Praxis is 'a fundamental defining element of human existence and an essential precondition for attaining freedom' (Glass, 2001, p.16).

As I will elucidate in the forthcoming sections, at the core of praxis lies the integration of reflection and action. In the context of ethical GCE, praxis is defined as ethical, self-aware, responsive, and accountable action. In praxis, theory is intricately interwoven with both theory and action. Consequently, it can be understood as a series of cycles that encompass doing, reflecting on one's actions, and formulating theories based on these experiences. Praxis can never be rigidly procedural or predefined since it is context-sensitive and takes shape in specific situations.

Fostering students' critical thinking mindset through praxis is pivotal for examining moral and ethical dilemmas, which span both local and global contexts. This approach empowers learners to cultivate their perspectives and engage in addressing fundamental issues like social justice, racism, refugee crises, workers' rights, and gun violence, underscoring the understanding that merely 'knowing without acting is insufficient' ([8]Bosio, 2024, January 11).

Hence, ethical GCE places a strong emphasis on educators' role in guiding students to cultivate cyclical knowledge, encompassing reflection and action (action-reflection/reflection-action), concerning society and its intricate socio-economic processes. This approach to ethical GCE aims to create an environment where educators and students collaborate to critically analyse their reality and devise transformational strategies. Central to this process is the embracing of multiple perspectives, a vital component of engaging in praxis within the realm of ethical GCE.

Furthermore, this engagement is nurtured through the establishment of genuine collaborative efforts. Students and individuals from historically marginalised communities can come together to address contemporary local and global issues such as racism, social equity, and justice. They engage in critical reflections on ethical values and participate in discussions that have, at least potentially, a lasting impact on community settings and college campuses alike. This

---

[8] Bosio (2024, January 11). The Emergence of the Ethically-Engaged University [Book Launch Speech]. Centre for Global Higher Education (CGHE), London, United Kingdom. www.youtube .com/watch?v=z3tZ8a5ZaN0

dynamic creates a platform for collective action, fostering the pursuit of morally upright, just, and enduring societal change in everyday life (Bosio & Waghid, 2023a).

2.6 Critical Reflection

The critical reflection element of ethical GCE entails developing students' ability to assess injustices and inequalities rooted in their social circumstances. This involves a critical examination of political, social, economic, and racial or gender disparities (Giroux & Bosio, 2021).

Educators play a pivotal role in helping students comprehend the reasons behind the denial of opportunities and resources within their communities. They achieve this by guiding students through a process of critical reflection. In this ethically and socially justice-oriented approach, students are encouraged to contemplate the fundamental connection between their oppressive living conditions and the systems that perpetuate these injustices. As individuals engage in higher levels of critical reflection, they can draw connections between oppressive practices of the past and those that persist in the present (Bosio & Waghid, 2022c).

However, reflection alone, without corresponding action, leads to a purely intellectual engagement. The development of critical consciousness in ethical GCE requires not only critical reflection but also proactive action for the 'common good' (Bosio & Torres, 2019). Here, the common good embodies a foundational concept of social and political morality, underscoring the importance of contributing to the betterment of society at large. Ethical GCE encourages learners to combine critical reflection with meaningful actions aimed at addressing societal injustices and advancing the cause of justice and equality.

2.7 Critical Action

Critical action within the context of ethical GCE embodies a proactive stance, where educators motivate students to actively confront and challenge the injustices they encounter through engagement in political processes and social justice activism. This proactive involvement can take various forms, including participation in organised activities and social movements, such as clubs, political groups, or public demonstrations, as well as individual socio-political actions like signing petitions or communicating with politicians (Bosio, 2023a). As articulated by Freire (2000, p. 73), critical action 'results from the intervention in the world as transformers of that world'.

An ethical educator recognises that students' perceptions of themselves, others, and the prevailing societal inequalities are profoundly shaped by their civic engagement and socio-political actions. Ethical educators understand that when students actively confront oppressive circumstances, a newfound awareness of themselves, their peers, and the local socio-political landscape emerges (Giroux & Bosio, 2021). Hence, an ethical educator enables students to cultivate the identity of engaged, proactive, and ethical global citizens. These individuals embody civic responsibility, foster a deep social connection to their community, and harbour confidence in their capacity to enact change for the common good (Bosio & Schattle, 2021a, 2021b).

Reclaiming marginalised and undervalued identities constitutes just one facet of the transformative shift in self-perception that occurs during this empowerment process put forward by the ethical GCE. To achieve this, ethical educators must foster students' sense of community, enhance their accountability for future challenges, and bolster their self-efficacy. Ultimately, within the framework of ethical GCE, critical action instils in students the belief that they have the capacity to make a difference and promote social justice and equity as engaged, informed global citizens.

Critical introspection and action serve as essential components, forging a connection between the reflective self and others in social interactions. Critical self-reflection involves a thorough examination of one's assumptions, biases, and perspectives, with a focus on shifting attention away from the individual and towards the mechanisms of oppression and injustice (Bosio, 2020).

The concept of ethical GCE revolves around nurturing learners' critical consciousness and self-awareness, fostering an understanding of complex social issues, and cultivating both individual and collective commitment to reflective, ethical practice. This process, when coupled with subsequent action, constitutes one of the foundational pillars of ethical GCE.

2.8 Reflexive Dialogue

Reflective dialogue within ethical GCE aligns with inclusive scholarship, analogous to what Dempsey and Barge (2014) term 'democratic conversation'. Ethical GCE embraces the recognition of diversity. This approach exemplifies a commitment to social justice, equitable material conditions and positioning, and resource equity.

In ethical GCE, reflexive dialogue involves the realms of politics, society, economics, and history. Ethical GCE seeks to enhance students' understanding of cultural variations and critically examines intricate relationships, power dynamics, and hierarchies.

This approach to ethical GCE is aligned with Torres and Bosio's (2019) pedagogical vision, which positions GCE as an educational theory of the common good rooted in Freirean critical pedagogy aimed at fostering students' socio-political perspectives (Bosio & Torres, 2019; Torres & Bosio, 2020a, 2020b). Specifically, Torres and Bosio (2019, 2020b) discuss a critical and ethical turn in GCE – one in which the three core dimensions of (a) reflexive dialogue, (b) praxis for societal change and (c) students' critical consciousness development are interrelated and valued, and issues of power and resistance become essential in pedagogy.

Hence, one of the central dimensions of ethical GCE is a transformative, democratic, and respectful form of reflexive dialogue. Reflexive dialogue as a dimension of ethical GCE encompasses educators assisting students in their specific struggles to decide who they have been and what they will become. Hence, the reflexive dialogue component of ethical GCE involves a guided and interactive process of introspection. In this process, educators assist students in exploring their feelings and values through the lens of the subjects they have discussed with their peers.

From this perspective, ethical GCE has the potential for transformation as it enables students to articulate their values and motivations to themselves through sincere and respectful interactions with the other. Herewith, ethical GCE serves as a catalyst for critical consciousness-raising, allowing students to discover and express aspects of their identity that may remain unexplored without the opportunity provided by the educator. Consequently, genuine, problem-posing oriented GCE becomes imperative (Freire, 1973). It calls upon educators to:

- foster a comprehensive perspective that recognises a universal bond based on shared human traits, acknowledging that all members of our species share a common humanity. These bonds, theoretically at least, propel global citizens towards the aspiration of global peace, cooperation, and justice
- engage in open dialogues with students to cultivate shared values
- emphasise cultural diversity and the concept of the 'Other', while also critically examining various connections, disparities in privilege, and degrees of agency
- seek out and explore the concept of 'intersectionality' throughout the entire teaching process (Bosio & Waghid, 2022c).

When applied from this perspective, ethical GCE helps learners in critically understanding multiple relationships within local, national, and international communities.

Lastly, ethical GCE includes the encouragement of deliberate interactions among diverse peers, emphasising the promotion of intergroup dialogue. In ethical GCE, intergroup dialogue serves as an educational intervention designed to engage students across differences. From this standpoint, ethical GCE should facilitate dialogues that unite individuals from opposing identity groups (e.g., men and women, people of different races) (Bosio, 2023d; Zúñiga, Naagda, & Sevig, 2002).

Intergroup dialogue and its pedagogical objectives can be realised through ethical GCE either as a co-curricular activity or through university course credit. In practice, intergroup dialogues typically comprise eight to twelve meetings conducted over the span of a semester, involving twelve to eighteen participants, and led by two co-facilitators representing the identities relevant to the dialogue topic (Zúñiga, Naagda, & Sevig, 2002).

Intergroup dialogue is particularly well suited for encompassing cognitive, emotional, and behavioural dimensions of learning within the framework of ethical GCE. It nurtures a sense of social responsibility while encouraging active student engagement across cultural and societal divides, facilitating an enhanced understanding of social diversity and disparities.

2.9 Framing the Critical Principles of Ethical GCE

In framing the critical principles of ethical GCE (decolonialism, caring ethics, eco-critical views, critical consciousness, praxis, critical reflection, critical action, reflexive dialogue) (Figure 2), they span various pedagogical themes.

As exemplified in Figure 2, ethical GCE promotes diversity and decolonisation over neutral, universal subjectivities. This approach empowers students to critically analyse their beliefs, perspectives, and identities within the complex framework of both national and international systems (decolonialism). It encourages the concept of ethics of care, encouraging students to prioritise respect for individuals and uphold human rights as a foundational principle (caring ethics). It nurtures ecological consciousness, guiding students in scrutinising the injustices stemming from humanity's perception of itself as the supreme entity on Earth, thus aligning with the principles of eco-critical and eco-ethical pedagogy (ecocritical perspective). It cultivates a more holistic understanding of the world among students, encouraging awareness, and exposure to political and social contradictions. This process includes instilling intangible values like a profound sense of solidarity, respect for humanity, and the acknowledgement that our planet is our only home (critical consciousness).

Ethical GCE highlights the crucial need for educators to prioritise cultivating students' well-rounded understanding (reflection-action/action-reflection) of social structures and society. This involves fostering an environment where educators and students collaboratively engage in critical reflection on their reality, devising strategies for transformation (praxis). it underscores the

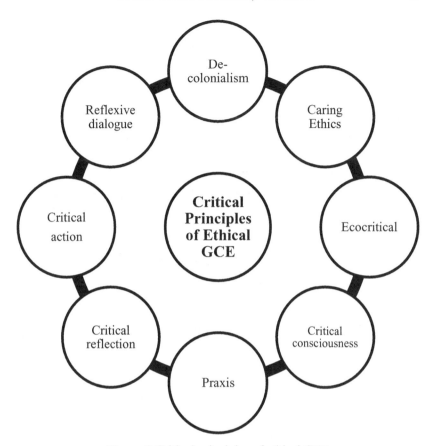

Figure 2 Critical principles of ethical GCE

importance of critical reflection, as educators guide students in understanding why their communities experience limited access to essential resources and opportunities. This process, oriented towards social justice, encourages students to explore the fundamental link between their oppressive living conditions and the structures perpetuating these injustices (critical reflection). It reflects a proactive approach, with educators inspiring students to actively address and challenge the injustices they encounter through engagement in political processes and social justice activism. This proactive involvement can manifest in various ways, including participating in organised activities and social movements (e.g., political groups, public demonstrations), as well as socio-political actions (e.g., signing petitions, communicating with politicians) (critical action).

Lastly, ethical GCE involves interactive and guided introspection, where educators facilitate deep discussions among students about their values and needs in connection with the topics they are exploring alongside their peers.

This process includes purposeful interactions among diverse groups of students, with a focus on fostering reflexivity and promoting social interaction (reflexive dialogue)

In closing, educators who adopt an ethical GCE approach encourage students to examine the root causes of poverty and global inequality. In doing so, they challenge the colonial interpretation of history that has often been used to politicise the past. Additionally, these educators help students comprehend macrostructural relationships and the injustices present in local and global justice systems.

This theoretically allows students to question the historical belief that neo-liberalism is the exclusive route to human development, as well as the notion that Western capitalism, knowledge, technology, and political systems such as liberal democracy are the sole valuable models.

3 Cosmopolitan Principles of Ethical GCE

In this section, I explore the cosmopolitan principles of ethical GCE entrenched in Rooted Cosmopolitanism, (a) openness to the 'Global Other' while rooted in the local and (b) deep dialogue; Universal Cosmopolitanism, fostering (c) compassionate imagination based on a view of the world in its entirety as a unity; and, Ground-Up Cosmopolitanism, promoting (d) 'balance' – the concept that both the local and global have equal importance.

Altogether, but with different variations, these cosmopolitan principles of ethical GCE recognise that every citizen of the globe, in theory, shares a universal morality. This shared morality is crucial for advancing ethical and democratic values (Appiah, 2006; Archibugi, 2002, 2008).

3.1 Rooted Cosmopolitanism

Ethical GCE supports local and global (glocal) humanitarian obligations and the significance of every human life. Yet, loyalty is very much rooted in locality – the local. Appiah's (2006) values of rooted cosmopolitanism inform an ethical GCE where educators aim at improving students' knowledge and values regarding ethical belief systems and practices, and the development of respect for difference with a particular reference to local dynamics.

3.1.1 Openness to the 'Global Other' while Rooted in the Local

In an ethical GCE informed by the values of rooted cosmopolitanism, educators assist learners in appreciating the cultures/practices of others. They help them recognise that neoliberalism alone is insufficient for orienting them in the direction of visions of human goodness. In line with this, McDonough and Feinberg (2003) propose 'affiliation liberalism', which has similarities with rooted cosmopolitanism, as a means of recognising the necessity of openness to the 'Global Other' while being rooted in the local.

What these two authors and Appiah (2006) imply in relation to my discussion on ethical GCE is that in this pedagogical approach, educators aim at fostering global citizens who acknowledge that they have cultural roots in their locality but are aware that growth cannot occur if its only foundation is a blind loyalty to the nation-state.

3.1.2 Deep Dialogue

Deep dialogue involves engagement with the philosophy and experience of the Other. Appiah (2006) suggests that 'Cosmopolitans suppose that all cultures have enough overlap in their vocabulary of values to begin a conversation' (p. 57) (see also my preceding discussion on 'reflexive dialogue'). Appiah (2006) implies that humans are connected to cosmopolitanism based on two categories: the local and the universal. By engaging in deep dialogue, educators can help learners appreciate differences, the values of others and their importance.

In the realm of faith, dialogue is a topic that is often discussed, yet its instructional aspects, particularly within the context of GCE, remain largely unexplored. Yet, examining dialogue from the perspective of GCE yields valuable insights (Bosio, 2021a; Bosio & Guajardo, 2024a).

Many educators find themselves ill-equipped to teach in a truly dialogical manner, often due to their own experiences in graduate school or the educational environments in which they operate. Nevertheless, dialogue, particularly as I conceptualise it in this discussion on ethical GCE, is an 'ongoing, evolving communication exchange that allows us to obtain a more comprehensive understanding of the world, ourselves, and each other' (Burbules, 1993, p. 8). As Buber (1955, p. 58) notes 'the relation in education is one of pure dialogue' (Buber, 1955, p. 58).

From this angle, ethical GCE underscores the importance of broadening perspectives through dialogue and the willingness to absorb knowledge from the perspectives of the other.

3.2 Universal Cosmopolitanism

An ethical GCE grounded in the values of universal cosmopolitanism nurtures learners' compassionate imagination. When students are open to discovering other cultures and nations and recognise that we share the same future, they are more likely to cooperate nationally and internationally to address local and global challenges, such as climate change, pandemics, and conflicts. This dedication extends to value-creation and the common good (Bosio & Guajardo, 2024b; Nussbaum, 2002, 2005).

3.2.1 Compassionate Imagination

Educators promoting ethical GCE foster learners' compassionate imagination, which extends through the encouragement of global citizens to put themselves in the position of others far different and to have the capacity to 'be an intelligent reader of that person's story, and to understand the emotions and wishes and desires someone so close might have' (Nussbaum, 2005, p. 46).

Educators hereby support students in understanding that developed nations and their citizens are morally obliged, under a central pillar of cosmopolitanism, to uphold universal human rights (Osler & Starkey, 2005). Ethical global citizens, in acknowledging that chance national borders have too much influence on the ways in which opinions and ideas are developed, will start to view the world in its entirety as a unity and thus participate in meaningful discussion regarding local and global issues, and cooperating to find their solutions.

This also connects with Archibugi's (2008, p. 144) notion of 'cosmopolitical democracy', which highlights the political significance of this battle: 'What distinguishes cosmopolitical democracy from other such projects is its attempt to create institutions which enable the voice of individuals to be heard in global affairs, irrespective of their resonance at home'. This is the idea of a feasibly-utopian civil society in which citizens have chances to contribute directly to making local and global choices, and applying ethical principles of democracy internationally (Archibugi, 2008, 2002; Bosio, 2022a, 2022b, 2022c; Popkewitz, 2008).

3.3 Ground-Up Cosmopolitanism

Cosmopolitanism from the ground up 'challenges stereotypical views of the cosmopolitan as an elite and rootless standpoint in the world' (Hansen, 2011, p. 10). Focusing more closely on the ways in which the educator perceives and interprets their environment, ethical GCE proposes a ground-up cosmopolitanism that, as with Appiah (2006), acknowledges both local and global connections. This ground-up cosmopolitanism represents 'an orientation in which people learn to balance reflective openness to the new with a reflective loyalty to the known' (Hansen, 2011, p. 1).

3.3.1 Balance: 'Think Globally and Act Locally'

In the discourse on ethical GCE, balance suggests an endeavour to 'think globally and act locally' or, conversely, 'to act globally but think locally'. Essentially, it emphasises the equal importance of both local and global issues and their profound interconnectedness. This emphasis is crucial, considering one major critique of notions of global citizenship is that it focuses on the global while neglecting the local, despite the profound relationship between the local and global – glocal.

The concept of global citizenship is sometimes perceived as 'a new paradoxical policy slogan' that might serve as 'a theoretical concept that travels well' (Mannion et al., 2011, p. 1), yet it often operates (either inadvertently or deliberately) as a marketing tool rather than as a pedagogical practice grounded in principles of local and global social justice.

Hence, balance requires educators to recognise several characteristics of global citizenship, some tangible, and some intangible. In the context of ethical GCE, these include, for instance, refusing affiliation with any party or movement that uses ideology for the exclusion of others and comprehending the various ways in which we may learn from one another, particularly from local and Indigenous cultures, and the Global South (Bosio, 2022b, 2022c).

Educators implementing an ethical GCE from a ground-up perspective have an innate cosmopolitanism in that they are representative of a locality but are also willing to consider fresh perspectives and concepts. In designing an ethical GCE, educators attempt to assist both themselves and their learners by the development of a toolkit that allows for an improved understanding of cosmopolitanism through participatory processes (Bosio, 2023c, 2023d).

Such an ethical GCE encourages educators to foster students' ability to reflect, read, interact, and listen mindfully. Within the framework of ethical GCE, the emphasis on mindful teaching underscores the vital role of educators in classrooms. It stresses that educators should inherently be oriented towards cosmopolitanism, influencing both their classroom practices and the implementation of ethical GCE that focuses on exploring new possibilities, embracing embodiment, fostering observation, welcoming differences, and cultivating compassion (McCown, Reibel, & Micozzi, 2010).

3.4 Framing the Cosmopolitan Principles of Ethical GCE

In summarising the cosmopolitan principles of ethical GCE (openness to the 'Global Other' while rooted in the local, deep dialogue, compassionate imagination, and balance), they span various pedagogical themes (Figure 3).

As elucidated in Figure 3:

- encouraging the global citizen to recognise the necessity of openness to the 'Global Other' through deep dialogue while being ingrained in the local (rooted cosmopolitanism)
- fostering in the global citizen a compassionate imagination and a view of the world in its entirety as a unity; thus, encouraging participation in meaningful

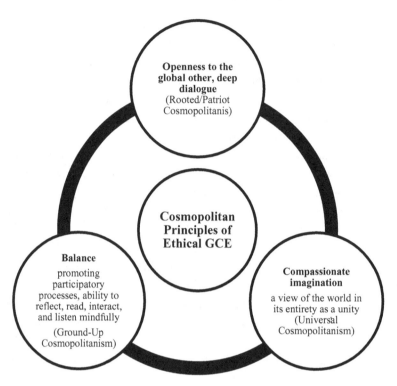

Figure 3 Cosmopolitan principles of ethical GCE

discussion regarding glocal problems and cooperating to find their solutions (universal cosmopolitanism)

• nurturing the ability to reflect, read, interact, and listen mindfully while being entrenched in both the glocal (ground-up cosmopolitanism).

These cosmopolitan principles within ethical GCE highlight that educators play a role beyond simply transmitting knowledge (Bosio & Gregorutti, 2023a, 2023b, 2023c). Ethical GCE educators find themselves in a distinctive position, where they can lead in promoting ethical values and knowledge within their respective fields, navigating unexplored territories in the realm of science (Barnett, Parry, & Coate, 2011; Bosio & Waghid, 2023a, 2023b). They should possess the ability to cultivate students whose moral foundation is rooted in personal experiences and the capability to tackle challenges at both local and global levels (Bosio & Waghid, 2022a, 2022b, 2022c, 2022d).

In this context, educators who implement ethical GCE play a crucial role in instilling in students a sense of shared humanity and a recognition of the inter-connectedness that binds societies together. From this standpoint, I propose that the concept of 'difference' forms the bedrock of ethical GCE.

Herewith, educators assist students in developing a cultural understanding of cosmopolitanism, even within the digital age of information and communication technologies, amidst our super-complex societies (Bosio, 2023b; Bosio & Schattle, 2021a, 2021b; Bosio, Torres & Gaudelli, 2023; Bosio et al., 2023). Concurrently, cosmopolitanism, as discussed in relation to ethical GCE, represents an ethically guided imperative that moulds a moral perspective towards the entire planet.

4 Humanistic Principles of Ethical GCE

In this section, I examine the humanistic principles of ethical GCE. Specifically: (a) global moral consciousness, (b) autonomy and carefulness, and (c) empowering humanity. As discussed in the preceding, the notion of moral obligation rooted in cosmopolitanism is a central component of ethical GCE.

However, ethical GCE goes beyond this. It emphasises the development of 'a moral consciousness to act for the good of the world, an awareness of other perspectives, and a vision of oneself as part of a global community of humanity as a whole' (Dill, 2013, p. 2).

Human development is intrinsically linked to ethical global citizenship education (GCE). Various perspectives, including cultural, psychological, evolutionary, and sociological (Veugelers & Bosio, 2021), philosophical (Noddings, 2018), and even spiritual (Ikeda, 2010), can be employed to analyse this process.

Based on a humanistic standpoint, ethical GCE provides learners with an education that enables them to act and reflect critically (praxis), understand the complexities of their surroundings (epistemology), and identify with them (ontology).

From this perspective, ethical GCE plays a pivotal role in nurturing students into global citizens who are not only aware of their own humanity but also connected to the broader world.

Ethical GCE is therefore closely intertwined with the concept of a compassionate culture (Noddings, 2005), humanisation (Freire & Macedo, 1995), and a caring community (Harding & Ikeda, 2013). Furthermore, it is associated with elements of global moral consciousness, carefulness, and the empowerment of humanity (Bosio, 2022c).

4.1 Global Moral Consciousness

The concept of global moral consciousness within ethical GCE encompasses the development of a humanistic consciousness that transcends national, ethnic, geographical, and religious boundaries. This kind of consciousness has gained prominence among progressive educators (Bosio & Waghid, 2022a, 2022b).

From this perspective, I argue that educational standards should incorporate the building of moral solidarity within a single human community. I suggest that educators who embrace ethical GCE should not only raise awareness of local and global issues such as hunger, poverty, and climate change but also nurture moral ideals for a universal community (Bosio & Waghid, 2022c, 2022d).

Hence, the global moral consciousness aspect of ethical GCE entails acknowledging humanity as the fundamental level of community. The moral obligation to act in the planet's best interests, guided by three principles: understanding different perspectives, recognising a unified humanity as the primary community, and having a moral conscience to promote the world's well-being.

In line with this perspective, ethical GCE aims to promote moral principles and foster individuals who perceive, at least ideally, the world as a universal community without borders, where members care for one another and the environment. From this angle, ethical GCE nurtures students who not only think globally but also act locally in ways that promote global consciousness, embodying the ideal of being 'morally conscious citizens' in the cosmopolitan age (Veugelers & Bosio, 2021).

4.2 Autonomy and Carefulness

Ethical GCE seeks to foster students' autonomy and carefulness. Autonomy in this context does not imply that a morally conscious global citizen lives in isolation from society; rather, it pertains to how educators facilitate the interactions of global citizens with others, emphasising the importance of empathy and consideration for fellow individuals (Bosio & Schattle, 2021a, 2021b).

The foundation of humanity serves as the basis for morally upright global citizens to potentially unlock their full potential as human beings through self-reflection and dialogue, enabling them to lead lives in harmony with others based on an ethical framework and to support others in pursuing meaningful lives (Bosio, 2023c).

However, achieving autonomy and developing carefulness is not necessarily inherent for global citizens. It emerges from interactions within social frameworks. The enhancement of autonomy and carefulness is deeply intertwined with dynamics related to society, culture, and politics (McLaren & Bosio, 2022).

The cultivation of autonomy and carefulness is not a straightforward journey. Rather, it is an interactive progression influenced by social and political power dynamics that educators promote through ethical GCE.

From this perspective, educators support learners who understand that acquiring autonomy and carefulness is vital for social, cultural, and political advancement. This suggests that, akin to how autonomy is inseparable from humanity, carefulness is indivisible from the collective social, cultural, and political pursuit of social justice.

4.3 Empowering Humanity

In the pursuit of empowering humanity, ethical GCE seeks to play a crucial role in facilitating personal growth and development for every global citizen. While the terms 'empowering humanity' and 'collective emancipation' are often used interchangeably due to their shared mission of combating inequality, within this discussion on ethical GCE, they do have subtle distinctions.

Collective emancipation primarily focuses on rectifying power imbalances among various groups while empowering humanity encompasses all aspects of human life, extending beyond the realm of politics (Bosio & Olssen, 2023).

The concept of empowering humanity through ethical GCE can be delineated into three key dimensions. Firstly, a *personal dimension*. Individuals aspire to live with dignity, asserting control over their lives. It involves self-empowerment, self-awareness, and personal agency. Secondly, an *interpersonal dimension*. It recognises the inherent human desire for harmonious and responsible coexistence with others. It emphasises the importance of fostering relationships built on mutual respect and support within communities. Lastly, a *socio-political dimension*. The socio-political aspect of ethical GCE entails the collective effort to create a more compassionate society characterised by principles of equality, diversity, and justice. This involves both giving and receiving support from the local community. Such engagement necessitates navigating and, when necessary, reforming existing social structures.

The empowering humanity principle of ethical GCE entails a complex political component that inherently involves challenges. As individuals become more engaged in and aware of their political and social roles, there may be conflicts between personal autonomy and societal responsibilities (Veugelers & Bosio, 2021).

Ethical GCE advocates for a balanced approach that encourages both personal empowerment and social consciousness. It recognises that achieving the goal of empowering humanity necessitates collective efforts that span personal, interpersonal, and socio-political dimensions.

4.4 Framing the Humanistic Principles of Ethical GCE

In summarising the humanistic principles of ethical GCE (global moral consciousness, autonomy and carefulness, and empowering humanity) (Figure 4), they span various pedagogical themes.

As exemplified in Figure 4:

- Acknowledging a united humanity as the foundational community level and having a moral conscience to strive for global improvement (global moral consciousness)

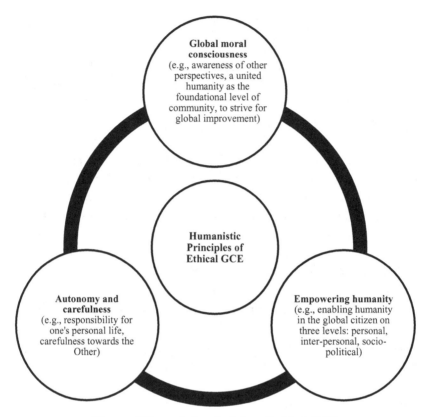

Figure 4 Humanistic principles of ethical GCE

- fostering learners' autonomy by increasing their responsibility for their personal lives and promoting carefulness towards others (autonomy and carefulness)
- enabling humanity in global citizens across personal, interpersonal, and socio-political levels (empowering humanity).

Inspiring empathetic concern for others is fundamental to ethical GCE. This concern for others plays a central role in shaping relationships within the broader human community (Veugelers & Bosio, 2021).

5 Value-Creating Principles of Ethical GCE

In this section, I examine the value-creating principles of ethical GCE. Specifically: (a) wisdom, courage and compassion, (b) beauty, gain and good, (c) affinity (Oikeiôsis), (d) respect, (e) sense of mission, protection, greater and multifaceted self, and (e) kōsen-rufu/world peace.

The notion of value-creation (Soka in Japanese), originated with Japanese educator Tsunesaburo Makiguchi (1871–1944) and underwent further refinement by Japanese Buddhist philosophers, authors, and advocates of nuclear disarmament, Josei Toda (1900–1958) and Daisaku Ikeda (1928–2023). It is within this framework that the pedagogy of value-creation has its roots.

Makiguchi's vision of value-creation in education serves as one of the guiding principles of ethical GCE, empowering teachers to nurture global citizens actively engaged in both local and global communities (Bosio, 2024; Bosio & Guajardo, 2024a).

Rooted in principles of value-creation, ethical GCE focuses on cultivating students' capacity to find meaning in their own existence and contribute to the well-being of others (Ikeda, 2010). It aims to foster the development of emancipated and informed global citizens, extending its impact beyond those situated in the Global North or from affluent backgrounds (Bosio & Guajardo, 2024b).

At the core of ethical GCE entrenched in value-creation is the imperative to inspire students to not only acknowledge but also to identify and eradicate what Ikeda (1993, p. 2) refers to as 'the arrow of a discriminatory consciousness, an unreasoning emphasis on difference ... piercing the hearts of the people'. This central objective underscores the intent of ethical GCE to instil values that transcend discrimination and prejudice, towards wisdom, courage, and compassion.

5.1 Wisdom, Courage, and Compassion

Ethical GCE plays a pivotal role in nurturing the holistic development of global citizens, focusing on the cultivation of three essential value facets. Firstly, *wisdom*. Recognising the interconnectedness of all human lives is a core aspect of wisdom that ethical GCE promotes. This wisdom extends beyond learners recognising the interdependence of individuals and communities to encompass a broader understanding of global interconnectivity (Bosio & Guajardo, 2024a, 2024b).

Secondly, courage. Ethical GCE encourages learners to exhibit courage by embracing diversity and actively seeking to understand people from all walks of life. This entails a genuine effort to appreciate and respect the richness of cultural differences, fostering inclusivity and unity (Bosio, 2024).

Thirdly, compassion. Compassion is a fundamental value cultivated through ethical GCE, potentially enabling learners to transcend their own cultural boundaries. It involves the capacity to empathise with the suffering and challenges faced by individuals in diverse regions and nations. This empathy forms the basis for building connections and fostering a sense of shared humanity (Ikeda, 2010).

In addition to these three foundational facets, ethical GCE assists morally upright learners in cultivating a range of virtues, including:

- self-determination, it aims at encouraging learners to take charge of their own lives, make informed choices, and set meaningful goals for personal growth and development
- inventiveness, it involves fostering creative thinking and problem-solving skills to address complex global challenges and find innovative solutions
- affection, it promotes a sense of care, empathy, and emotional connection towards others, irrespective of their cultural backgrounds
- humanity-centeredness, it cultivates an overarching sense of placing humanity at the forefront of decision-making and actions, with a focus on contributing positively to the welfare of all people (Bosio, 2024).

5.2 Beauty, Gain, and Good

As I elucidated in the preceding, at the core of an ethical GCE based on the principles of Makiguchi's philosophy of value-creation lies a pursuit of true humanity, where human interaction with the environment serves as the well-spring of value creation itself. According to Makiguchi, value can only emerge through this dynamic engagement with one's surroundings (Bosio, 2024).

Makiguchi introduces three fundamental components of values that guide his perspective:

- beauty signifies the aesthetic appreciation and emotional resonance that arise from the sensory experiences within one's environment
- gain represents the measurement of a connection encompassing all of an individual's essential experiences and interactions. It captures the culmination of personal encounters and the value derived from them
- good pertains to the value that an individual's life contributes to the collective well-being of the social community. It represents the positive impact and contributions that an individual can make to society (Ikeda, 2010).

Makiguchi envisions these components as concentric circles of expansion, extending from an individual's life to the broader sphere of the community's life. This perspective underscores the interconnectedness of individual experiences and contributions to the collective good.

Interestingly, Makiguchi's concentric circle method bears artistic and historical resemblance to Hierocles' Circle Model of Identity (CMI). In Hierocles' CMI, individuals are conceptualised as concentric circles, with the innermost circle representing the self and subsequent circles encompassing extended family, local community, fellow citizens, and, ultimately, all of humankind.

Both Makiguchi and Hierocles' CMI models resonate with my conceptualisation of ethical GCE. They both emphasise the importance of recognising our shared humanity and the responsibilities that come with it, highlighting the role of individuals in contributing positively to the broader social fabric.

5.3 Affinity (Oikeiôsis)

Hierocles' CMI is significant in relation to my discussion on ethical GCE because it is an invitation for human beings to envision themselves as 'concentric circles', representing distinct spheres of connection and engagement (Figure 5).

As illustrated in Figure 5, Hierocles' CMI begins with the innermost circle, representing oneself. This is followed by concentric circles that encompass one's immediate or extended family, local community, fellow citizens, and, ultimately, the global community of all humanity.

Similarly, through the ethical GCE framework, learners are assisted in developing a natural inclination towards others – from 'self' to 'mankind as a whole' through the process of orientation and familiarity, a concept the Stoics referred to as 'Oikeiôsis'.

Ethical GCE promotes individuals' recognition of themselves as citizens not only of their local and national communities but also of the global community simultaneously.

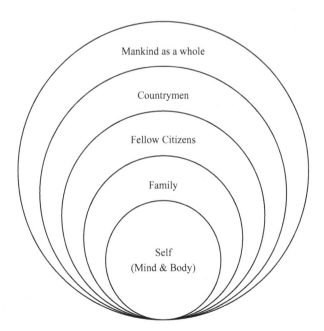

Figure 5 Hierocles' circle model of identity

Ethical GCE promotes a conceptualisation of society based on the idea of cross-cultural dialogue as a means to foster the development of a broader moral consensus. This involves principles of respect, a sense of mission for contributing to the common good, and protection of human rights towards a greater and multifaceted self.

5.4 Respect, Sense of Mission, Protection, Greater and Multifaceted Self

In ethical GCE, fostering students' sense of respect is concerned with encouraging them to adopt an outlook on life that values the inherent worth and potential of each individual. This principle emphasises treating every person with dignity and esteem.

Developing in students a sense of mission means inspiring them to embrace a purpose aimed at contributing to the betterment of society. This entails leading a profoundly compassionate life and striving to make a positive impact. Protection involves instilling in students a lifelong commitment to safeguard humanity and uphold this pledge throughout their lives. This commitment underscores the responsibility to protect and preserve the well-being and rights of all people. Lastly, greater self entails encouraging students to live a selfless life characterised by a commitment to assisting others while striving to cultivate a compassionate attitude. This principle emphasises personal growth, empathy, and the development of an adaptable character capable of connecting with people from all walks of life (Bosio, 2024).

These principles collectively form a comprehensive framework that not only guides students in their understanding of ethical GCE but also empowers them to actively embody the values and behaviours of ethical and value-creating global citizens. Through these principles, educators can play a pivotal role in shaping individuals who are not only conscious of their roles within society but also dedicated to making a positive difference in the world.

5.5 Kōsen-rufu (広宣流布) – World Peace

Ethical GCE advocates for the cultivation of 'kōsen-rufu' (広宣流布), a term found in the Japanese version of the Lotus Sutra. It underscores the importance of fostering understanding and cooperation among individuals from diverse backgrounds, spiritual traditions, and perspectives.

Kōsen-rufu, when translated literally, means 'to proclaim and disseminate the Buddha's teachings'. However, it has evolved to encompass the broader aspiration of achieving 'world peace', particularly influenced by the Lotus Sutra and the teachings of Japanese Buddhist priest Nichiren Daishonin (1222–1282).

One of the primary objectives of ethical GCE is to inspire students to work towards the establishment of world peace, with a focus on creating more peaceful societies as stepping stones.

This goal can be pursued by advocating for the gradual prohibition and elimination of nuclear weapons, responding ethically and compassionately to global refugee crises, and nurturing a culture that upholds and respects human rights (Bosio, 2024; Ikeda 2017).

5.6 Framing the Value-Creating Principles of Ethical GCE

The value-creating principles of ethical GCE encompass various pedagogical principles (Figure 6).

As indicated in Figure 6, these principles encompass:

- wisdom, acknowledging the interconnectedness of all human lives, courage (accepting difference and striving to understand diverse peoples), and compassion (empathising with the suffering of others beyond one's cultural context)

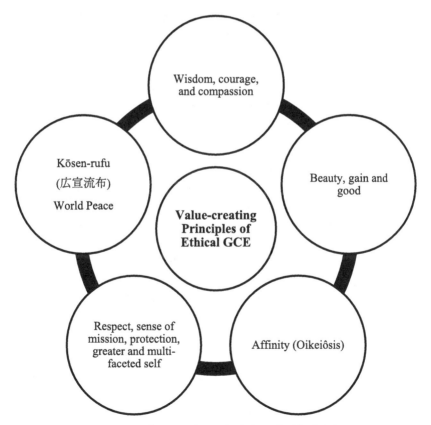

Figure 6 Value-creating principles of ethical GCE

- beauty, gain, and good serve as indicators of an ongoing sensory response within an individual. They assess the entirety of a relationship's essential experience for the individual and its impact on the collective well-being of society
- oikeiôsis, orientation and familiarisation
- respect, a view of life that respects the sanctity and dignity of every human being, fostering societal betterment and protection
- greater and multifaceted self, living altruistically and easily relating to others
- kōsen-rufu/world peace, encouraging learners to contribute to the establishment of more peaceful societies.

Sharma (2018/2020) and Bosio and Guajardo (2024) have recently discussed an additional set of values associated with ethical GCE, suitable for incorporation into formal, non-formal, and informal education across diverse subjects and disciplines. These values encompass a sense of interdependence, common humanity, and a global perspective; recognition of climate change as a concern for global citizens; dedication to reflective, dialogic, and transformative learning; commitment to sustainable development through intercultural lenses; belief in the capacity for social self-actualisation to generate value; and acknowledgement of peace and non-violence as foundational to the human rights agenda.

The work of Sharma (2018/2020) and Bosio and Guajardo (2024) is particularly important in this discussion on ethical GCE as it seeks to find points of contact with UNESCO's (2014) GCE framework and critical GCE theorists (e.g., Vanessa Andreotti, Sharon Stein, Dalene Swanson, Karen Pashby and others) in a way that shows potential for being more critically oriented.

6 Transformative Principles of Ethical GCE

In this section, I examine the transformative principles of ethical GCE. This selective review of literature on transformative learning theory (Mezirow, 2000) and the transformative learning model for service learning (Kiely, 2004) suggests that the principles underpinning educators' transformative approaches to ethical GCE must entail an emphasis on developing self-awareness.

6.1 Transformative Learning Theory

An understanding of the transformative principles of ethical GCE begins with a brief analysis of Mezirow's (1996) transformative learning theory. Mezirow (1996, p. 162) characterised transformative learning as based on communication between humans, in which 'learning is understood as the process of using a prior interpretation to construct a new or revised interpretation of the meaning of one's experience in order to guide future action'.

This process takes place within a frame of reference: a unique but culturally and environmentally sensitive ensemble of perspectives that underlie and inform the actions, values, and assumptions of any given individual.

During the transformation period, this frame of reference undergoes a paradigmatic shift as the individual incorporates her/his own experience, producing, according to Mezirow (1996, p. 163):

> a more fully developed (more functional) frame of reference ... one that is more: (a) inclusive, (b) differentiating, (c) permeable, (d) critically reflective, and (e) integrative of experience. The duration of this transformation is variable; for some, it is an accumulation of experiences, while for others, it is triggered or accelerated by a single formative life event such as bereavement, relationship breakdown, or retirement, all of which cause learners to question the meaning of their life and the assumptions around which they have built it.

In the context of this discussion on ethical GCE, a key aspect of transformative learning involves educators actively facilitating the transformation of global citizens' perspectives. This transformation is achieved through a critical examination of their pre-existing preconceptions and beliefs, followed by a deliberate and conscious redefinition of their understanding of the world, often accomplished through the cultivation of innovative strategies related to concepts of meaning and experience (Clark & Wilson, 1991).

Transformative learning has a trio of dimensions that inform an ethical GCE, these being:

- an interpersonal environment offering emotional support that ensures that every student is able to have equal access to all necessary information and that the information should be shared
- extending students' personal capacity for critical reflection, internal dialogues, discernment, and self-awareness
- students both individually and as a cohort should have the flexibility to offer a critical approach to their learning experiences (Elias, 1997).

6.2 Transformative Learning Model for Service-Learning

Richard Kiely is one of the scholars who has made an empirical study of the transformative learning theory. Kiely's (2005) work created a theoretical framework that explains the ways in which students encounter transformative learning within service learning.

It is important for this discussion on ethical GCE that I concisely explore the correlation between transformative learning and service learning, as teaching methodologies intended to create ethical global citizens frequently gain support and improvements from links between local and global communities (Bamber et al., 2016) that allow students to develop and learn intellectually, morally, personally, and socially. Participating in service-learning programmes can be transforming for students spiritually, culturally, personally, intellectually, politically, and morally (Kiely, 2005).

The transformative learning model for service-learning proposed by Kiely (2005) is important for the examination of ethical GCE as the preparation of students for global citizenship via international service-learning has gained increasing popularity amongst academics (Bamber & Bullivant, 2013).

Service-learning experiences may transform perspectives when learners are assisted by the 'unfamiliar' in their questioning of the 'familiar'. One example would be how socio-linguistic assumptions could be transformed through interrogation of an individual's most foundational societal beliefs so that their comprehension of what a social problem is can be completely changed, along with the ways in which they perceive the measures required for their solution (Bosio, 2022a, 2022b).

In the same way, when students are immersed in service-learning contexts, they may experience challenges to their personal values and stereotypical thinking and be exposed to unfamiliar concepts that may be contradictory to their existing beliefs. By critically reflecting personally, intellectually, politically, morally, culturally, and spiritually, students become de-familiarised, that is, they abandon preconceived notions and set aside familiarities (Bosio, 2020).

6.3 Deconstruction of Learners Established Mental Habits

An ontology emphasising the profound importance of existential transformation in learners, encompassing not only how they engage with the world but also how they perceive and experience it, is a fundamental prerequisite for ethical GCE (Bosio & Schattle, 2021; Bamber, Lewin & White, 2017).

As such, ethical GCE embraces comprehensive concepts of transformational learning that extend beyond Mezirow's primary emphasis on deconstructing deeply ingrained assumptions (Mezirow, 2000). This broader educational philosophy involves an epistemology that includes the deconstruction of established mental habits.

The influential writings of Mezirow (2009, 2003) regarding transformative learning offer a separation between the human experience as lived and the ways in which we construct meanings. Experience counts before reflection, and then later experience becomes learning. With holistic conceptions of ethical GCE, knowledge derives from modes of being, not the other way around.

This perspective demands that educators implement an ethical GCE that is less about acquiring knowledge and more concerned with offering support to the individual as they transform their modes of being, exemplified by the term 'critical being'. Such progressive experiences inevitably encompass affective and cognitive dissonances that work on both the unconscious and conscious levels.

6.4 Framing the Transformative Principles of Ethical GCE

As I frame the transformative principles of ethical GCE, namely transformative learning theory (Mezirow, 1996), the transformative learning model for service-learning (Kiely, 2004), and holistic transformative teaching and learning (Bamber, Lewin, & White, 2017), we can see that this can cover several pedagogical themes (Figure 7).

As illustrated in Figure 7:

- ethical GCE encourages learners undergo a fundamental shift in their frames of reference through reflective examination of their assumptions and beliefs,

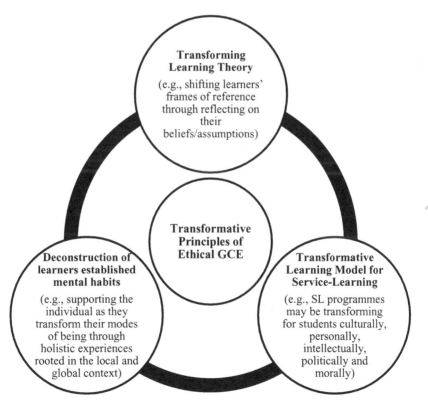

Figure 7 Transformative principles of ethical GCE

and they intentionally reshape their perception of their environment by developing new approaches (Mezirow's transformative learning theory)
- ethical GCE might benefit form service-learning programmes as they may be transforming students culturally, personally, intellectually, politically, and morally (transformative learning model for service-learning)
- ethical GCE seeks to assist the learner as they transform their modes of thinking and being through holistic experiences ingrained in the local and global context (deconstruction of learners established mental habits) (Bosio & Schattle, 2021a, 2021b).

Ethical GCE advocates for fostering mutual interaction among individuals from diverse backgrounds and encourages the recognition of differences that honour and respect ethno-cultural identities (Mezirow, 1996).

Excessively highlighting the 'otherness' of individuals we encounter can potentially reinforce prejudices and power imbalances. Conversely, concentrating solely on commonalities may lead to the overlooking of significant variations in the human experience (Bosio & Waghid, 2023a, 2023b). This challenge is addressed by acknowledging the importance of developing an 'otherwise' perspective as individuals learn about pluralism and diverse perspectives (Stein & Andreotti, 2021).

6.5 Existing Criticism and Concluding Remarks

In closing, it is worth noting that the transformative, cosmopolitan, value-creating, humanistic, and critical GCE orientations I discussed in relation to ethical GCE often face criticism in the literature. For example, initiatives promoting transformative GCE, such as service-learning projects, despite their benefits in assisting communities, may sometimes neglect ethical engagement, reciprocity, and the values of the communities they aim to serve.

Similarly, Miller (2002) asserts that the cosmopolitanism advocated by Appiah (2006), Nussbaum (2002), and Hansen (2011), whether transformative or rooted, would necessitate the creation of a 'world government', which could inherently adopt imperialist tendencies, potentially abolishing existing local cultural differences. Bhambra (2016) adds that cosmopolitanism lacks direct confrontation with Eurocentrism and fails to offer explicit challenges to the prevailing neoliberal narrative.

Humanistic GCE positions are criticised for being perceived as superficial slogans or marketing tools rather than effective tools for social justice education (Stein, 2015). Andreotti (2011) coined the term 'soft GCE' to describe an approach solely based on humanistic and moral obligations. An additional critique of the humanistic GCE stance, which also applies to value-creating

GCE, is presented by Stein (2015). She contends that these approaches might be considered somewhat individualistic because they 'often concentrate on global relationships at the individual level rather than at a structural level, such as through an emphasis on intercultural understanding' (Stein, 2015, p. 245).

Critiques of these GCE perspectives primarily arise from critical theorists such as Sharon Stein, Karen Pashby, and Vanessa Andreotti. However, there has also been criticism of these critiques, arguing that global relationships are often oversimplified into oppressor–oppressed dichotomies, neglecting the complexities of these issues (Rizvi, 2007).

Acknowledging these critiques, leading GCE scholars Pashby and Andreotti (2016) highlight the need to recognise the intersections between critical orientations, liberal, and neoliberal discourses. They emphasise the importance of understanding how these discourses perpetuate colonial systems and suggest exploring new possibilities beyond existing frameworks (Pashby et al., 2020).

This prompts the question of whether we should approach ethical GCE through the lens of 'value-pluralism' (also known as ethical-pluralism). Value-pluralism acknowledges that different ethical domains are grounded in a variety of knowledge(s) and values. This perspective aligns with Webster's (2023) research, which argues that it might be more beneficial for students to learn how to critically evaluate diverse knowledge(s) and values rather than having educators impose a specific set of beliefs.

Considering ethical GCE within the framework of value-pluralism serves to clarify the role of the global citizen and provides a basis for making normative, ontological, and aspirational conclusions.

In the subsequent section, I will explore how this diversity of principles can be integrated to create a pedagogical framework that embraces value-pluralism and is well suited for ethical GCE. While the framework may not be exhaustive, its intent is to offer educators and practitioners practical insights on effectively applying the GCE ethical concepts discussed thus far.

7 Envisioning an Ethical GCE Reinforced by Value-Pluralism

7.1 Introduction

In this concluding section, I aim to discuss the various perspectives presented on ethical GCE to enhance the reader's understanding of its breadth and relevance in today's globalised world.

I present value-pluralistic ethical GCE as shaped by a multitude of values, incorporating a diverse range of knowledge spanning human development, sustainability, dialogue, and social transformation. Rooted in critical, cosmopolitan, humanistic, value-creating, and transformative principles, this approach offers pathways for ethical teaching and learning.

Value-pluralistic ethical GCE breathes life into concepts such as global citizenship, critical consciousness development, and sustainable development by integrating both Western and non-Western theoretical frameworks (Bosio, 2023b, 2023c; Bosio & Waghid, 2022a). It fosters enriched discussions on social and environmental justice, encompassing topics like climate change, conservation, and biodiversity. While presenting opportunities for advancing sustainable societies and the common good, value-pluralistic ethical GCE also faces challenges. It aims to guide community life towards fairness, justice, and sustainability, with a focus on Peace, People, and Planet (Bosio & Torres, 2019).

Given the current climate of social and environmental challenges, value-pluralistic ethical GCE goes beyond job market skills to emphasise ethical values-creation. It prioritises holistic education and research aimed at transforming learners' lives and fostering an appreciation for global interconnectedness (Bosio, 2023a). Educators play a crucial role in this transformative journey, nurturing learners who can contribute meaningfully to society and the planet. Embracing pedagogy as a journey of growth, educators can inspire contributions to global well-being in an interconnected world (Bosio, 2023b).

Shifting teaching and learning objectives towards ethical pedagogy is further enhanced by value-pluralism, offering a promising framework for reimagining educational models. Value-pluralistic ethical GCE holds the potential to evolve into a transformative platform for cooperation and solidarity, aligning with UNESCO's (2021) report *Reimagining Our Futures Together: A New Social Contract for Education*[9].

7.2 Value-Pluralistic Ethical Global Citizenship Education Framework: Five Key Themes

Herewith, I introduce a framework for further exploration and enhancement of ethical GCE teaching and learning, encompassing five key themes (Figure 8):

- **Theme 1:** Promoting Social Justice, Post/Decolonialism, Caring Ethics, Eco-critical Perspectives, Critical Consciousness, Action and Reflection, and Reflexive Dialogue for Sustainability in Teaching and Learning
- **Theme 2:** Fostering Learners' Openness to the 'Global Other', Compassionate Imagination, and Ability to Reflect Mindfully

---

[9] The full report is available here: https://unesdoc.unesco.org/ark:/48223/pf0000109590

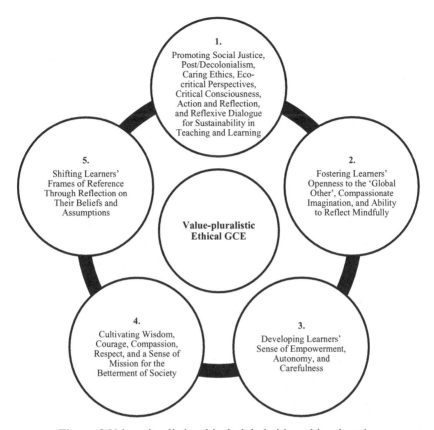

Figure 8 Value-pluralistic ethical global citizenship education

- **Theme 3:** Developing Learners' Sense of Empowerment, Autonomy, and Carefulness
- **Theme 4:** Cultivating Wisdom, Courage, Compassion, Respect, and a Sense of Mission for the Betterment of Society
- **Theme 5:** Shifting Learners' Frames of Reference through Reflection on Their Beliefs and Assumptions.

As illustrated in Figure 8, the five themes are interconnected with the sections discussed earlier in this Element:

7.3 Promoting Social Justice, Post/Decolonialism, Caring Ethics, Eco-critical Perspectives, Critical Consciousness, Action and Reflection, and Reflexive Dialogue for Sustainability in Teaching and Learning

As illustrated in Figure 8, ethical GCE is strengthened by value-pluralism. It fosters transformative change across various levels (individual, community, and systemic), while bridging humanity and pedagogy. It amplifies the role of the global citizen towards a global ethic based on principles of social justice, post/decolonialism, caring ethics, eco-critical, critical consciousness, action and reflection, and reflexive dialogue.

Specifically, it seeks to nurture the growth of critical and moral consciousness among all learners – not solely those who are white, affluent, and situated in the Global North. Its objective is to cultivate students who feel accountable to society and are prepared to contribute to social justice as they transition beyond education.

In the introductory section of this Element, I elaborate on how analysing the economic, social, and environmental factors fuelling unjust power dynamics (e.g., gender inequality, healthcare, social class, and income gap) can provide an optimal ethical pedagogical approach that 'challenges prevailing neoliberal concepts regarding the connections between globalisation and education and guides learners towards social justice' (Bosio, 2021b, p. 1).

Doing so reduces, at least to some extent, any feelings of powerlessness students may have towards the task of making a sustainable impact on society and our shared planet. For instance, gaining an understanding of how bias and oppressive systems impede societal progress can motivate learners from various backgrounds to recognise the advantages of education for promoting social justice (El-Amin et al., 2017).

As students' critical consciousness strengthens, they become less likely to 'blame the victim' and more driven to understand the myriad interconnected causes at play, the institutional oppression that underpins them, and the historical progression of these complex conditions (Kelly & Varghese, 2018).

Herewith, I infer that promoting global citizenship and critical consciousness, facilitated by value-pluralistic ethical GCE enriched by critical pedagogy, social justice (Giroux & Bosio, 2021), critical GCE (McLaren & Bosio, 2022), and culturally relevant/responsive pedagogy (Jackson & Boutte, 2018), requires integrating the aim of nurturing learners who are motivated to be respectful and engaged individuals within a value-pluralistic ethical GCE framework. In pursuing this objective, value-pluralistic ethical GCE places emphasis on a vision for sustainability rooted in ethical values while upholding principles of social justice.

Building on the above concepts, I contend that value-pluralistic ethical GCE aims to offer high-quality scientific/academic education while emphasising social justice, humanity, ethics, and politics in its pedagogy. Herewith, learners are motivated to foster more reflective and responsible relationships and interactions within their communities, both locally and globally.

Therefore, I adopt an intrinsic-critical pedagogy concept within the framework of value-pluralistic ethical GCE knowledge and values. Dewey (1944) distinguishes between ends and means: instrumental knowledge/values and intrinsic knowledge/values, respectively. This concept is widely recognised in education, especially when examining how educational objectives are formulated and how they influence student motivation. Typically, within market-oriented and/or neoliberal educational frameworks, behaviours may prioritise ultimate goals (e.g., exam success and workplace readiness) over deeper educational objectives (e.g., profound learning and critical knowledge).

Value-pluralistic ethical GCE empowers students to become critical agents tasked with actively questioning and negotiating the connections between education and social change, theory and practice, critical analysis, and the common good.

With an ethical GCE informed by such perspectives, no student will emerge accepting of social injustices. For instance, students will develop the mindset to challenge racism, xenophobia, homophobia, sexism, slavery, human trafficking, stereotyping, religious, gender, and disability discrimination.

In order for educators to adopt value-pluralistic ethical GCE, they need to thoroughly consider how politics and culture intersect with pedagogy. McLaren and Bosio (2022) offer a comprehensive description of how I define ethical GCE: in the context of socio-political practices with an emphasis on social justice politics.

Value-pluralistic ethical GCE champions decoloniality and diversity over neutral universal subjectivities, empowering learners to scrutinise their preconceptions, positions, and identities in the context of complex local and global structures (decolonialism). It promotes caring ethics, urging learners to prioritise the well-being of individuals and uphold human rights as fundamental values (caring ethics). It fosters ecological consciousness, urging learners to scrutinise the injustices arising from humanity's perception of its supremacy on Earth (eco-critical). It puts forward a holistic understanding of the world among students, fostering awareness and exposure to political and social contradictions. This process instils in learners intangible values such as profound solidarity, respect for humanity, and recognition of our planet as our only home (critical consciousness).

Value-pluralistic ethical GCE emphasises the crucial role of educators in prioritising the cultivation of students' comprehensive understanding of social structures and society. This entails creating an environment where educators and students engage in collaborative critical reflection on their reality and develop strategies for transformation (praxis). It highlights the significance of critical thinking as educators guide students in comprehending why their communities face restricted access to vital resources and opportunities. This progression, geared towards social justice, prompts students to delve into the fundamental connection between their oppressive living conditions and the structures perpetuating these injustices (critical reflection).

Value-pluralistic ethical GCE embodies a proactive approach, as educators encourage students to actively address and challenge encountered injustices through engagement in political processes and social justice activism. This proactive involvement can take various forms, including participation in organised activities and social movements like clubs, political groups, or public demonstrations, as well as individual socio-political actions such as signing petitions or communicating with politicians (critical action).

Lastly, value-pluralistic ethical GCE entails guided and interactive introspection, where educators prompt learners to discuss their needs and values within the context of topics explored with their peers. This involves deliberate interactions among diverse peers, emphasising the promotion of reflexivity and active engagement with others (reflexive/intergroup dialogue).

Educators who adopt a value-pluralistic ethical GCE approach motivate students to analyse the root causes of global inequalities and poverty, challenging the traditional colonial interpretation of historical events by examining the politicised, ahistorical portrayal of poverty. They also assist students in understanding concepts such as inequality, justice, and macrostructural relationships, empowering them to recognise and potentially critique the historical notion that human development follows only one path – the neoliberal approach – and that Western capitalism, knowledge, technology, and forms of government (e.g., liberal democracy) are the sole valuable models.

Educators would strive to foster learners' understanding of how social, political, and economic inequalities are critically assessed, particularly in relation to how a neoliberal agenda perpetuates colonial-era inequalities. This understanding should equip graduates to demonstrate the varied and multifaceted effects of globalisation, and to grasp how current cultural, economic, political, and social norms are heavily influenced by the cultural hegemony of imperial power structures (Giroux & Bosio, 2021).

Educators would also nurture eco-critical thinking among ethical global citizens. This would empower them to 'recognize an anthropocentric worldview – that is, one that takes humans as the reference point – and how that worldview is culturally constituted and maintained' (Lupinacci, 2017, p. 22), also referred to as ego-tistical, fostering a more sustainable worldview. Lupinacci (2017) defines an eco-tistical worldview as one that 'does not explicitly perpetuate human-supremacy' (p. 21), enabling the global citizen to discern ways in which the injustices, exploitation, and inequality resulting from human-centrism can be confronted on political and ethical grounds.

Educators who embrace a value-pluralistic ethical approach to GCE play a crucial role in nurturing students' holistic understanding of the world and fostering critical consciousness. By cultivating awareness of political and social contradictions, educators instil intangible values such as profound solidarity, respect for humanity, and recognition of our planet as our shared home (Bosio, 2023a).

However, this task is not without its challenges, particularly in the Global South. For instance, Angyagre (2022) examines GCE within a Ghanaian university context, emphasising the importance of addressing the impacts of globalisation on African societies, particularly in Ghana. Awad and Carbajal (2022) explore GCE through the lens of democratic citizenship education in Egypt and Mexico. They observe that only a limited number of teachers employ conflict dialogue pedagogies to navigate discussions on contentious issues, enhancing students' democratic skills within culturally relevant contexts. Lastly, Hong's (2022) research investigates GCE implementation in Chinese secondary schools, focusing on leadership roles. Through the analysis of school principals, her study reveals that authoritative leadership often impedes ethical and critical GCE by perpetuating asymmetric power dynamics and promoting patriotic values. These studies suggest that a value-pluralistic ethical approach to GCE must be conceptualised and implemented to support educators in prioritising the development of students' comprehensive understanding of societal structures through reflective-action methods.

By fostering environments for collaborative critical reflection and praxis, educators guide students to grasp the root causes of limited access to resources and opportunities in their communities, with an emphasis on social justice (Bosio & Olssen, 2023).

7.4 Fostering Learners' Openness to the 'Global Other', Compassionate Imagination, and Ability to Reflect Mindfully

Aligned with the concepts outlined above, value-pluralistic ethical GCE aims to enrich the principles of rooted/patriot cosmopolitanism (e.g., Appiah, 2006), universal cosmopolitanism (e.g., Nussbaum, 2005), and ground-up cosmopolitanism (e.g., Hansen, 2011) towards what Bosio (2020) describes as the 'altruistic and authentic self'.

A primary objective of value-pluralistic ethical GCE is to assist educators and learners in fostering an appreciation for being receptive to the 'Global Other' through dialogue while remaining grounded in the local context (rooted/patriot cosmopolitanism). This entails nurturing in the global citizen a compassionate imagination and a holistic worldview, promoting active participation in meaningful conversations about global challenges and collaborative efforts to address them (universal cosmopolitanism). Additionally, it involves cultivating the capacity for reflection, reading, interaction, and attentive listening while maintaining strong ties to both local and global communities (ground-up cosmopolitanism).

Viewed through the lens of value-pluralistic ethical GCE, educators play a role that extends beyond simple knowledge transmission. They are uniquely positioned to engage in research related to their teaching subjects, to remain at the forefront of knowledge on relevant issues, and to navigate the inherent uncertainties of science (Barnett, Parry & Coate, 2001). As highlighted by Nussbaum (2002), educators have the capacity to nurture students whose moral compass is rooted in personal experiences and the ability to confront challenges encountered at local and global levels. Within this framework, value-pluralistic ethical GCE contributes to shaping learners' understanding of shared humanity and fosters an appreciation for the connections that unite communities.

From this standpoint, I propose that the concept of difference is fundamental to value-pluralistic ethical GCE, emphasising the importance for students to foster a cultural understanding of cosmopolitanism within the broader global context. At the same time, cosmopolitanism serves as a crucial ethical imperative guiding a moral perspective towards the planet, nurturing the growth of an altruistic and authentic self that enhances not just the individual's life but also the lives of others, contrasting with a rigid, individualistic self.

I suggest that when students and teachers embrace altruism and solidarity, going beyond the notion of the individualistic self, they can help shift egotistical societies towards altruistic and sustainable societies. This doesn't necessarily demand complex actions. It could include students minimising food waste, expanding learning into the community, and advocating for equality (Bosio, 2024; Bosio & Guajardo, 2024a, 2024b).

As this unfolds, learners scrutinise and reassess their daily habits and behaviours. They become more inclined to pursue sustainable ethics and foster value-creating societies. As learners move beyond self-serving actions, they are better prepared to aim for a 'contributive life', actively engaging in community-based initiatives aimed at realising what the Japanese pedagogue Tsunesaburo Makiguchi (1871–1944) referred to as the 'life of the greater unity' for individual and collective happiness (Bethel, 1989, p. 48).

7.5 Developing Learners' Sense of Empowerment, Autonomy, and Carefulness

Value-pluralistic ethical GCE empowers humanity, calling upon educators to facilitate the personal advancement of every global citizen. While the term is sometimes used interchangeably with collective emancipation due to their shared aim of combating inequality, there is a nuanced distinction. Collective emancipation focuses on equalising power relations between groups, whereas empowering humanity extends beyond politics to encompass all facets of human behaviour.

Value-pluralistic ethical GCE empowers humanity within the global citizen on three fronts: personal, interpersonal, and socio-political. At the personal level, individuals seek to lead dignified lives while exerting control over their circumstances. The interpersonal dimension recognises the innate desire for harmonious and responsible coexistence, involving both giving and receiving support from one's community. Finally, the socio-political dimension of citizenship involves striving to build a fairer society marked by equality, diversity, and justice, often necessitating reform within existing social structures.

The political aspect of empowering humanity is inherently intricate. As individuals become involved in political and social matters, there is a tension between autonomy and social awareness – both essential aspects within value-pluralistic ethical GCE.

Moreover, value-pluralistic ethical GCE involves nurturing learners' global moral consciousness, autonomy, and carefulness, thus contributing to the empowerment of humanity. This entails cultivating an understanding of diverse viewpoints, acknowledging a shared humanity as the bedrock of community, and fostering a moral compass to drive actions for global betterment. Additionally, it includes enhancing students' autonomy and carefulness by deepening their sense of responsibility for their personal lives and fostering empathy towards others.

In closing, value-pluralistic ethical GCE advocates for empathy, cosmopolitanism, and social activism to nurture engaged and proactive global citizens (Bosio & Waghid, 2022b) and supports collective human advancement towards realising our shared humanity (United Nations, 2020). The implementation of value-pluralistic ethical GCE requires educators to embrace and champion human diversity while acknowledging the interconnectedness and intersectionality present at all levels of education (Veugelers & Bosio, 2021).

7.6 Cultivating Wisdom, Courage, Compassion, Respect, and a Sense of Mission for the Betterment of Society

Value-pluralistic ethical GCE nurtures learners' wisdom, acknowledging the interconnectedness of all human lives, courageously embracing diversity, and striving to understand people from various backgrounds. It also cultivates compassion, enabling individuals to transcend their cultural context and empathise with the suffering of people in different regions and countries.

Value-pluralistic ethical GCE advocates for respect. It cherishes the sanctity of life and honours the dignity of every human being. This includes a sense of mission (for societal improvement), protection (for humanity), a heightened sense of self (embracing altruism), and a multi-faceted self (facilitating easy rapport with others).

From this perspective, educators advocate for the development of all three dimensions of value: wisdom (recognising the interconnectedness of all human lives), courage (embracing diversity and seeking to understand people from diverse backgrounds), and compassion (being able to empathise with the suffering of individuals in other regions and nations beyond one's own cultural context) (Ikeda, 2010). In this framework, educators implementing value-pluralistic ethical GCE also facilitate the cultivation of principles like empowerment, creativity, affection, and a concern for humanity among ethical global citizens.

Value-pluralistic ethical GCE advocates for negotiation to occur between human hearts, bridging spiritual legacies and standing in solidarity with those different from us, to foster a global concept of kōsen-rufu (広宣流布), a term found in the Japanese translation of the Lotus Sutra. Kōsen-rufu means to declare and widely propagate the teachings of the Buddha. Nevertheless, the term kōsen-rufu has evolved to symbolise world peace rooted in the Lotus Sutra and the Buddhist teachings of the Japanese Buddhist priest Nichiren Daishonin (1222–1282).

Within a value-pluralistic ethical GCE framework, one of the primary objectives of educators is to inspire learners to pursue world peace, thereby nurturing more peaceful societies. This may entail initiatives such as advocating for the gradual prohibition and elimination of nuclear weapons, addressing the refugee crisis ethically, and fostering a culture of human rights (Harding & Ikeda, 2013; Ikeda, 2017).

Value-pluralistic ethical GCE integrates elements of value-creating education proposed by the Japanese educator Makiguchi's (1871–1944) pedagogical philosophy. This perspective translates into a core set of value-creating pedagogical principles that educators assist learners develop. The goal is to nurture ethical and value-creating global citizens. These principles encompass:

- respect, embracing a viewpoint that honours the sanctity of life and acknowledges the dignity of every human being
- sense of mission, pursuing a mission for societal improvement, fuelled by compassion
- protection, dedication to safeguarding humanity and living a life committed to fulfilling this duty

- greater-self, living altruistically, serving others, and striving to establish a more expansive sense of self
- multifaceted self, being adept at relating to others, maintaining a willingness to gain experiences and learn throughout life, and offering optimal solutions to diverse situations (Bosio, 2024).

Value-pluralistic ethical GCE also embraces an additional set of values associated with value-creating education, which can be integrated into formal, non-formal, and informal educational settings across various subjects and disciplines (Bosio, 2024).

These values include recognising interdependence, acknowledging shared humanity and a global perspective, being aware of climate change as global citizens, committing to reflective, dialogic, and transformative learning, dedicating to sustainable development through intercultural viewpoints, believing in social self-actualisation through creating value, and acknowledging peace and non-violence as crucial to the human rights agenda (Bosio & Guajardo, 2024a, 2024b).

7.7 Shifting Learners' Frames of Reference through Reflection on Their Beliefs and Assumptions

Finally, value-pluralistic ethical GCE requires an ontology that highlights the importance of learners undergoing existential changes, impacting both their existence in the world and their perceptions of it. Consequently, value-pluralistic ethical GCE integrates concepts of transformative learning, building upon Mezirow's emphasis on deconstructing ingrained assumptions (Mezirow, 2000), where the epistemology involves dismantling mental habits.

Mezirow's (2003, 2009) influential writings on transformative learning delineate the distinction between lived human experience and the construction of meanings. He posits that experience precedes reflection, and through this iterative process, experience evolves into learning.

In holistic views of value-pluralistic ethical GCE, knowledge stems from ways of existence rather than the other way around. This perspective calls for educators to implement a value-pluralistic ethical GCE that prioritises supporting individuals in transforming their ways of being, rather than solely focusing on acquiring skills for the global job market. This transformation involves experiencing both affective and cognitive dissonances, which operate at both unconscious and conscious levels (Bosio, 2020).

Value-pluralistic ethical GCE seeks to reshape learners' perspectives by encouraging them to reflect on their beliefs and assumptions, thereby consciously redefining their worldview through the development of new approaches, influenced by Mezirow's (2009) transformative learning theory. It provides support for learners as they undergo holistic transformations in their ways of being, drawing from experiences rooted in both local and global contexts (holistic transformation).

7.8 Conclusion

This section has proposed a vision for strengthening ethical GCE through a value-pluralistic conceptual framework based on five overarching themes: (1) Promoting Social Justice, Post/Decolonialism, Caring Ethics, Eco-critical Perspectives, Critical Consciousness, Action and Reflection, and Reflexive Dialogue for Sustainability in Teaching and Learning; (2) Fostering Learners' Openness to the 'Global Other', Compassionate Imagination, and Ability to Reflect Mindfully; (3) Developing Learners' Sense of Empowerment, Autonomy, and Carefulness; (4) Cultivating Wisdom, Courage, Compassion, Respect, and a Sense of Mission for the Betterment of Society; and (5) Shifting Learners' Frames of Reference Through Reflection on Their Beliefs and Assumptions.

These themes were exemplified by integrating dynamic approaches to ethical GCE presented by the author of the Element. The themes have been consolidated into a comprehensive framework fortified by value-pluralism. Though not exhaustive, value-pluralistic ethical GCE serves a distinct purpose by providing educators, learners, and policymakers with a broad spectrum of educational perspectives rooted in ethical values and a forward-thinking vision that is not exclusively dependent on the mechanisms of service delivery and neoliberalism. Instead, value-pluralistic ethical GCE requires integrating various types of knowledge and values, blending elements of critical, cosmopolitan, humanistic, value-creating, and ethical pedagogies (e.g., critical awareness, respectful relationships, reflective dialogue, environmental sustainability, wisdom, and social equity). Crucially, value-pluralistic ethical GCE leverages congruence with value-pluralism to achieve flexibility within its interconnected dynamics and multiple ethical perspectives that coexist.

When educators assist learners in adopting a value-pluralistic ethical GCE approach, it empowers them to appreciate cultural, religious, and philosophical diversity. Pedagogical methods that strive to nurture ethically and critically conscious individuals, as advocated by Freire (2000), emphasise the significance of critical awareness backed by respectful and participatory dialogue and reflection. Similarly, value-pluralistic ethical GCE embraces the three Ps: Peace, People, and Planet (Bosio & Torres, 2019). These include recognising the planet as our shared home, fostering world peace as a collective cultural pursuit, and promoting harmonious coexistence with mutual respect and dignity. This vision imagines a future where individuals can embrace and stand in solidarity with those from diverse cultures and identities.

Value-pluralistic ethical GCE will be the subject of further scrutiny by future researchers aiming to develop a more comprehensive understanding of the educational methodologies and learning objectives essential for promoting effective ethical global citizenship and fostering human flourishing.

In this context, the proposed value-pluralistic ethical GCE is rooted in key concepts such as global citizenship, values-based education, transformative learning, humanistic approaches, critical pedagogy, critical consciousness, and sustainable development. It is further enriched by inner transformation, dialogic learning, reflexivity, and creative coexistence, all of which engage learners in the construction and re-construction of more just, peaceful and sustainable societies, for, as Shaull (2000, p. 34) suggests in his foreword to the *Pedagogy of the Oppressed* (Freire, 2000):

> there is no such thing as a neutral education process. Education either functions as an instrument which is used to facilitate the integration of generations into the logic of the present system and bring about conformity to it, or it becomes the 'practice of freedom', the means by which men and women deal critically with reality and discover how to participate in the transformation of their world.

7.9 Limitations

Envisioning value-pluralistic ethical GCE, as discussed here, will have some limitations and is not beyond scrutiny. Such paradigms often emphasise foundational understanding and, given the incorporation of numerous complex issues, require a significant focus on 'utopian ideals' – though I prefer the term 'feasibly utopian ideals' – without necessarily conducting in-depth analyses of curricular and policy implications.

They may also overlook the importance of diverse regional or national cultures. Consequently, any paradigm for classifying and defining pedagogical thought and method, including the value-pluralistic ethical GCE proposed here, is bound to face scrutiny.

Yet, to contrast mechanistic, conveyor-belt, and market-driven approaches with value-pluralistic ethical GCE, we must continually redefine its objectives to advance students according to ethical and values-based perspectives, aligning with qualities integral to democratic progress. I believe it is imperative to offer a comprehensive overview of these objectives, especially within educational institutions globally dedicated to fostering ethical and sustainable global citizenship.

7.10 Recommendations for Future Research

The incorporation of ethical values and knowledge within GCE presents a valuable area for future research exploration. As the world evolves, it becomes increasingly important for students to graduate with a comprehensive understanding of their ethical responsibilities as global actors.

However, despite its potential significance, little investigation has been conducted into the influence of GCE, particularly concerning how it fosters students' ethical values and knowledge. Moving forward, it is crucial for policymakers, educators, and researchers to collaborate in promoting the ethical GCE agenda and identifying potential areas for future research.

In what follows, I offer a few final recommendations to guide these efforts. Such recommendations are not deemed to be exhaustive, and they are open to critique and further enhancement.

7.10.1 Research Recommendations

More longitudinal studies are needed to examine the long-term effects of ethical GCE on student outcomes, including attitudes, behaviours, and civic engagement. Utilising mixed-methods approaches provides comprehensive data on the impact of ethical GCE interventions. Additionally, exploring the influence of contextual factors such as cultural norms, socio-economic status, and school environment on the effectiveness of ethical GCE practices enhances our understanding of its broader implications. Collaboration with practitioners and policymakers is crucial to ensure that research findings are translated into actionable recommendations for educational practice and policy, facilitating the integration of ethical GCE into mainstream education.

7.10.2 Policy Recommendations

Allocating resources and funding to support the development and implementation of ethical GCE initiatives within educational systems is critical. Secondly, collaboration with relevant stakeholders, including government agencies, non-governmental organisations (NGOs), and international bodies, is crucial to establish guidelines and standards for ethical GCE practices. Lastly, encouraging the inclusion of ethical GCE components in teacher training and professional development programmes is vital to ensure educators are equipped to effectively integrate ethical considerations into their teaching practices.

7.10.3 Pedagogical Recommendations

It is important to integrate ethical GCE content across various subjects and grade levels to ensure comprehensive coverage. Additionally, incorporating experiential learning opportunities, such as social justice-oriented service-learning projects and community engagement activities, can reinforce ethical values and principles. Moreover, fostering a supportive and inclusive learning environment that encourages open dialogue, critical thinking, and reflection on ethical issues is essential. Lastly, providing opportunities for students to apply ethical decision-making skills in real-world contexts through case studies, simulations, and role-playing exercises enhances their understanding and application of ethical principles.

7.10.4 Collaborative Efforts

It is essential to facilitate interdisciplinary collaborations between educators, researchers, policymakers, and community stakeholders to advance ethical GCE initiatives. Establishing networks and forums (both online and face-to-face) for knowledge exchange can promote sharing of 'best practices' in ethical GCE implementation. Encouraging international collaboration and comparative research is vital to identify cross-cultural variations in the impact of ethical GCE on student outcomes. Additionally, fostering partnerships between schools, universities, and community organisations can create opportunities for experiential learning and civic engagement, enriching the educational experience and promoting active and ethical global citizenship.

It is hoped that by implementing these proposed recommendations, stakeholders can collaborate to advance the ethical GCE agenda and generate empirical evidence to guide future practice and policy decisions in the realm of global citizenship.

References

Abram, D. (1999). A More Than Human World. In A. Weston (Ed.), *An Invitation to Environmental Philosophy* (pp. 17–42). Book Section, New York: Oxford University Press.

Andreotti, V. (2006). Soft Versus Critical Global Citizenship Education. *Development Education, Policy and Practice, 3*, 83–98.

Andreotti, V. (2011). *Actionable Postcolonial Theory in Education.* Abingdon.

Angyagre, S. E. (2022). Conceptions of Global Citizenship Education in an African University Curriculum. In E. Bosio, & Y. Waghid (Eds.), *Global Citizenship Education in the Global South* (pp. 127–151). Leiden: Brill. https://doi.org/10.1163/9789004521742_008.

Appiah, A. (2006). *Cosmopolitanism: Ethics in a World of Strangers.* New York: W.W. Norton.

Archibugi, D. (2002). Demos and Cosmopolis. *New Left Review* (2nd Series), *13* (January/February), 24–38.

Archibugi, D. (2008). *The Global Commonwealth of Citizens: Toward Cosmopolitan Democracy.* Princeton: Princeton University Press.

Awad, Y., & Carbajal, P. (2022). Democratic Citizenship Education as an Instance of Global Citizenship Education. In E. Bosio, & Y. Waghid (Eds.), *Global Citizenship Education in the Global South* (pp. 152–176). Leiden: Brill. https://doi.org/10.1163/9789004521742_009.

Bamber, P. (2015). Becoming Other-Wise: Transforming International Service-Learning through Nurturing Cosmopolitanism. *Journal of Transformative Education, 13*(1), 26–45.

Bamber, P., Bullivant, A., & Stead, D. (2013). Measuring Attitudes towards Global Learning among Future Educators in England. *International Journal of Development Education and Global Learning, 5*(3), 5–27.

Bamber, P., Bullivant, A., Glover, A., King, B., & McCann, G. (2016). A Comparative Review of Policy and Practice for Education for Sustainable Development/Education for Global Citizenship (ESD/GC) in Teacher Education across the Four Nations of the UK. *Management in Education, 30*, 112–120. https://doi.org/10.1177/0892020616653179.

Bamber, P., Lewin, D., & White, M. (2017). (Dis-) Locating the Transformative Dimension of Global Citizenship Education. *Journal of Curriculum Studies, 50*(2), 204–230. https://doi.org/10.1080/00220272.2017.1328077.

Banks, J. A. (2017). Failed Citizenship and Transformative Civic Education. *Educational Researcher, 46*(7), 366–377. https://doi.org/10.3102/0013189X 17726741.

Banks, J. A. (2020). *Diversity, Transformative Knowledge, and Civic Education: Selected Essays.* New York: Routledge. https://doi.org/10.4324/9781 003018360.

Banks, J. A. (2021). *Transforming Multicultural Education Policy and Practice: Expanding Educational Opportunity.* New York: Teachers College Press.www.tcpress.com/transforming-multicultural-education-policy-and-practice-9780807766279.

Barnett, R., & Coate, K. (2005). *Engaging the Curriculum in Higher Education.* Buckingham: Open University Press.

Barnett, R., Parry, G., & Coate, K. (2001). Conceptualising Curriculum Change. *Teaching in Higher Education, 6*(4), 435–449. https://doi.org/10.1080/ 13562510120078009.

Berners-Lee, M. (2021). *There Is No Planet B: A Handbook for the Make or Break Years.* 2nd ed. Cambridge: Cambridge University Press. https://doi .org/10.1017/9781108900997.

Bethel, D. M. (Ed.) (1989). *Education for Creative Living: Ideas and Proposals of Tsunesaburo Makiguchi.* (A. Birnbaum, Trans.). Iowa: Iowa State University Press.

Bhabha, H. K. (1994). *The Location of Culture.* New York: Routledge.

Bhambra, G. K. (2016). Cosmopolitanism and Postcolonial Critique. In M. Rovisco, & M. Nowicka (Eds.), *The Ashgate Research Companion to Cosmopolitanism* (pp. 313–328). Abingdon: Routledge.

Bosio, E. (2020). Towards an Ethical Global Citizenship Education Curriculum Framework in the Modern University. In D. Bourn (Ed.), *Bloomsbury Handbook for Global Education and Learning* (pp. 187–206). London: Bloomsbury. www.bloomsburycollections.com/book/the-bloomsbury-handbook-of-global-education-and-learning/ch15-towards-an-ethical-global-citizenship-education-curriculum-framework-in-the-modern-university.

Bosio, E. (Ed.) (2021a). *Conversations on Global Citizenship Education: Perspectives on Research, Teaching, and Learning in Higher Education.* New York: Routledge. https://doi.org/10.4324/9780429346897.

Bosio, E. (2021b). Global Human Resources or Critical Global Citizens? An Inquiry into the Perspectives of Japanese University Educators on Global Citizenship Education, Springer, UNESCO-IBE Prospects, Comparative

Journal of Curriculum, Learning, and Assessment. https://doi.org/10.1007/s11125-021-09566-6.

Bosio, E. (2022a). Meta-Critical Global Citizenship Education: Towards a Pedagogical Paradigm Rooted in Critical Pedagogy and Value-pluralism. *Global Comparative Education: Journal of the World Council of Comparative Education Societies (WCCES)*, 6(2), 3–19. www.theworldcouncil.net/uploads/8/6/2/1/86214440/vol._6_no._2_gcejournal_of_the_wcces.pdf.

Bosio, E. (2022b). Embracing the Global South: Educators' Understanding on the Role of Global Citizenship Education in Brazil, South Africa, and Ghana. In M. Öztürk (Ed.), *Engagement with Sustainable Development in Higher Education: Sustainable Development Goals Series* (pp. 199–208). Cham: Springer https://link.springer.com/chapter/10.1007/978-3-031-07191-1_13.

Bosio, E. (2022c). Global Citizenship in Japanese Higher Education: Toward an Ethical Pedagogical Framework for Humanity Empowerment, Critical Moral Consciousness, Autonomy, and Carefulness. In W. O. Lee, P. Brown, A. L. Goodwin, & A. Green (Eds.), *International Handbook on Education Development in Asia-Pacific* (pp. 1–20). Singapore: Springer. https://doi.org/10.1007/978-981-16-2327-1_143-1.

Bosio, E. (2023a). The Ethically Engaged University for Critical Consciousness Development: A Six-dimensional Framework. In E. Bosio, & G. Gregorutti (Eds.), *The Emergence of the Ethically Engaged University*. New York: Springer – Macmillan: United States. https://link.springer.com/book/9783031403118.

Bosio, E. (2023b). Leveraging Online Teaching and Learning to Foster Critical Global Citizenship Education: Educators' Perceptions and Practices from Japan. *Journal of Creative Communications*, Sage. https://journals.sagepub.com/doi/10.1177/09732586231191027.

Bosio, E. (2023c). Global South University Educators' Perceptions of Global Citizenship Education: Reflective Dialogue, Social Change, and Critical Awareness. Springer, UNESCO-IBE Prospects Comparative Journal of Curriculum, Learning, and Assessment. https://doi.org/10.1007/s11125-023-09635-y.

Bosio, E. (2023d). Global Citizenship Education as a Reflexive Dialogic Pedagogy, *Citizenship Teaching & Learning*, 18(2), 177–194. https://doi.org/10.1386/ctl_00119_1.

Bosio, E. (2024). Value-Creating Education for Global Citizenship and Critical Consciousness Development: A Five-dimensional Framework. In E. Bosio, & M. Guajardo (Eds.), *Value Creating Education: Teachers Perceptions and Practice*. New York: Routledge. www.routledge.com/

Value-Creating-Education-Teachers-Perceptions-and-Practice/Bosio-Guajardo/p/book/9781032308555#.

Bosio, E., & Gregorutti, G. (Eds.) (2023a). *The Emergence of the Ethically Engaged University.* New York: Springer – Macmillan. https://link.springer.com/book/9783031403118.

Bosio, E., & Gregorutti, G. (2023b). The Ethically Engaged University as a Public Good Institution. In E. Bosio, & G. Gregorutti (Eds.), *The Emergence of the Ethically Engaged University.* New York: Springer – Macmillan. https://link.springer.com/book/9783031403118.

Bosio, E., & Gregorutti, G. (2023c). Envisioning an Ethically Engaged University Based on Value-pluralism. In E. Bosio, & G. Gregorutti (Eds.), *The Emergence of the Ethically Engaged University.* New York: Springer – Macmillan. https://link.springer.com/book/9783031403118.

Bosio, E., & Guajardo M. (Eds.) (2024a). *Value Creating Education: Teachers Perceptions and Practice.* New York: Routledge. www.routledge.com/Value-Creating-Education-Teachers-Perceptions-and-Practice/Bosio-Guajardo/p/book/9781032308555.

Bosio, E., & Guajardo M. (2024b). Envisioning a Value-Creating Education Strengthened by Value-pluralism. In E. Bosio, & M. Guajardo (Eds.), *Value Creating Education: Teachers Perceptions and Practice* (pp. 181–191). New York: Routledge. www.routledge.com/Value-Creating-Education-Teachers-Perceptions-and-Practice/Bosio-Guajardo/p/book/9781032308555#.

Bosio, E., & Olssen, M. (2023). Critical Global Citizenship: Foucault as a Complexity Thinker, Social Justice and the Challenges of Higher Education in the Era of Neoliberal Globalization – A Conversation with Mark Olssen. *Citizenship Teaching & Learning, 18*(2), 245–261. https://doi.org/10.1386/ctl_00123_1.

Bosio, E., & Schattle, H. (2021a). Educação para a cidadania global ética: do neoliberalismo a uma pedagogia baseada em valores, Revista Educação Unisinos, Educação Unisinos, *26*, 1–14. https://doi.org/10.4013/edu.2022.261.01.

Bosio, E., & Schattle, H. (2021b). Ethical Global Citizenship Education: From Neoliberalism to a Values-Based Pedagogy. *Prospects, 53*, 287–297. https://doi.org/10.1007/s11125-021-09571-9.

Bosio, E., & Torres, C. A. (2019). Global Citizenship Education: An Educational Theory of the Common Good? A Conversation with Carlos Alberto Torres. *SAGE-Policy Futures in Education, 17*(6), 745–760. https://doi.org/10.1177/1478210319825517.

Bosio, E., & Waghid Y. (Eds.) (2022a). *Global Citizenship Education in the Global South: Educators Perceptions and Practices.* Moral Development and Citizenship Education, Netherlands: Brill. https://brill.com/view/title/63195.

Bosio, E., & Waghid, Y. (2022b). Global Citizenship Education for Critical Consciousness Development: The Four Pillars of De-colonialism, Caring Ethics, Eco-critical Views, and Humanity Empowerment. In E. Bosio, & Y. Waghid (Eds.), *Global Citizenship Education in the Global South* (pp. 11–23). Leiden: Brill. https://doi.org/10.1163/9789004521742_002.

Bosio, E., & Waghid, Y. (2022c). Democratic Pluralistic Global Citizenship Education: Embracing Educators' Voices from the Global South. In E. Bosio, & Y. Waghid (Eds.), *Global Citizenship Education in the Global South* (pp. 284–294). Leiden: Brill. https://doi.org/10.1163/9789004521742_015.

Bosio, E., & Waghid, Y. (2022d). Embracing the Global South: Bringing Contemporary Academic Debate about 'Southern Theory' to Global Citizenship Education. In E. Bosio, & Y. Waghid (Eds.), *Global Citizenship Education in the Global South.* Leiden: Brill. https://doi.org/10.1163/9789004521742_001.

Bosio, E., & Waghid Y. (2023a). Cultivating Students' Critical Consciousness through Global Citizenship Education: Six Pedagogical Priorities. Springer, UNESCO-IBE Prospects Comparative Journal of Curriculum, Learning, and Assessment. https://link.springer.com/article/10.1007/s11125-023-09652-x.

Bosio, E., & Waghid, Y. (2023b). Global Citizenship Education as a Living Ethical Philosophy for Social Justice. *Citizenship Teaching & Learning, 18*(2), 151–158. https://doi.org/10.1386/ctl_00117_2.

Bosio, E., Torres, C. A., & Gaudelli, W. (2023). Exploring Values and Knowledge in Global Citizenship Education: Theoretical and Empirical Insights from Scholars Worldwide. Springer, UNESCO-IBE Prospects Comparative Journal of Curriculum, Learning, and Assessment. https://doi.org/10.1007/s11125-023-09658-5.

Bosio, E., Waghid, Y., Papastephanou, M., & McLaren, P. (2023). Critical and Creative Practices of Global Citizenship Education in the Digital Age of Information and Communication Technologies. Journal of Creative Communications, Sage. https://doi.org/10.1177/09732586231211397.

Buber, M. (1955). *Between Man and Man.* Boston: Beacon Press.

Burbules, N. (1993). *Dialogue in Teaching: Theory and Practice.* New York: Teachers College Press.

Clark, M. C., & Wilson, A. L. (1991). Context and Rationality in Mezirow's Theory of Transformational Learning. *Adult Education Quarterly, 41*(2), 75–91.

Dempsey, S. E., & Barge, J. K. (2014), Engaged Scholarship and Democracy. in L. L. Putnam, & D. K. Mumby (Eds.), *The SAGE Handbook of Organizational Communication: Advances in Theory, Research, and Methods* (pp. 665–688), 3rd ed., Thousand Oaks: Sage.

Dill, J. S. (2012). The Moral Education of Global Citizens. *Society, 49*, 541–546.

Dill, J. S. (2013). *The Longings and Limits of Global Citizenship Education: The Moral Pedagogy of Schooling in a Cosmopolitan Age.* New York: Routledge.

Dussel, E. (1977). Filosofia etica de la liberacion [Ethical philosophy of education]. 3rd ed., Vol. III. Niveles concretos de la etica latinoamericana. Ediciones Mega' polis.

Dussel, E. (1996). Modernity, Eurocentrism, and Trans-Modernity: In Dialogue with Charles Taylor. In E. Mendieta (Ed.), *The Underside of Modernity: Apel, Ricoeur, Rorty, Taylor, and the Philosophy of Liberation* (pp. 129–59). Mexico City: Humanities.

Dussel, E. (2019). Epistemological Decolonization of Theology. In M. P. Joseph, V. Hsu, & P. H. Huang (Eds.), *Wrestling with God in Context: Revisiting the Theology and Social Vision of Shoki Coe* (pp. 46–63). Mexico City: Fortress.

El-Amin, A., Seider, S., Graves, D., et al. (2017). Critical Consciousness: A Key to Student Achievement. *Phi Delta Kappan, 98*(5), 18–23.

Elias, D. (1997). It's Time to Change Our Minds: An Introduction to Transformative Learning. *ReVision, 20*(1), 2–7.

Freire, P. (1973). *Education for Critical Consciousness.* New York: Seabury.

Freire, P. (1994). *Pedagogy of Hope: Reliving Pedagogy of the Oppressed* (R. R. Barr, Trans.). New York: Continuum.

Freire, P. (2000). *Pedagogy of the Oppressed* (30th Anniversary ed.). New York: Continuum.

Freire, P. (2004). Pedagogia da tolerância [Pedagogy of tolerance]. New York: UNESP.

Freire, P., & Macedo, D. (1995). A Dialogue: Culture, Language, and Race. *Harvard Educational Review, 65*(3), 377–402.

Giroux, H. A., & Bosio, E. (2021). Critical Pedagogy and Global Citizenship Education. In E. Bosio (Ed.), *Conversations on Global Citizenship Education: Perspectives on Research, Teaching, and Learning in Higher Education* (pp. 1–10). New York: Routledge. https://doi.org/10.4324/9780429346897-1.

Glass, R. D. (2001). On Paulo Freire's Philosophy of Praxis and the Foundations of Liberation Education. *Educational Researcher, 30*(2), 15–25. https://doi.org/10.3102/0013189X030002015.

Guajardo, M. (2021). Global Citizenship Education and Humanism: A Process of Becoming and Knowing. In E. Bosio (Ed.), *Conversations on Global Citizenship Education: Perspectives on Research, Teaching, and Learning in Higher Education* (pp. 170–184). New York: Routledge .

Hansen, D. (2011). The Teacher and the World: A Study of Cosmopolitanism as Education. *Teacher Quality and School Development.* New York: Routledge.

Harding, V., & Ikeda, D. (2013). *America Will be! Conversations on Hope, Freedom, and Democracy.* Cambridge: Dialogue Path Press.

Hong, Y. (2022). Positioning Leadership Roles in Global Citizenship Education in China. In E. Bosio & Y. Waghid (Eds.), *Global Citizenship Education in the Global South* (pp. 177–197). Leiden: Brill. https://doi.org/10.1163/9789004521742_010.

Hooks, B. (1984). *Feminist Theory from Margin to Center.* Boston: South End Press.

Hooks, B. (1989). Talking Back: Thinking Feminist, Thinking Black. Boston: South End Press.

Ikeda, D. (1993, September 24). Mahayana Buddhism and Twenty-First Century Civilization. *Lecture Delivered at Harvard University.* www.daisakuikeda.org/sub/resources/works/lect/lect-04.html.

Ikeda, D. (2010). *A New Humanism: The University Addresses of Daisaku Ikeda.* New York: I. B. Tauris.

Ikeda, D. (2017). *The Global Solidarity of Youth: Ushering In a New Era of Hope.* www.sgi.org/about-us/president-ikedas-proposals/peace-proposal-2017/index.html.

Jackson, T. O., & Boutte, G. S. (2018). Exploring Culturally Relevant/Responsive Pedagogy as Praxis in Teacher Education. *The New Educator, 14*(2), 87–90. https://doi.org/10.1080/1547688X.2018.1426320.

Kelly, D. C., and Varghese, R. (2018). Four Contexts of Institutional Oppression: Examining the Experiences of Blacks in Education, Criminal Justice and Child Welfare. *Journal of Human Behavior in the Social Environment, 28*(7), 874–888. https://doi.org/10.1080/10911359.2018.1466751.

Kiely, R. (2004). A chameleon with a complex: searching for transformation in international service learning. *Michigan Journal of Community Service Learning,* Vol. Spring No. *2004*, 5–20.

Kiely, R. (2005). Transformative International Service Learning. *Academic Exchange Quarterly, 9*(1), 275–281.

Lupinacci, J. (2017). Addressing 21st Century Challenges in Education: An Ecocritical Conceptual Framework toward an Ecotistical Leadership in Education. *Impacting Education: Journal on Transforming Professional Practice*, 2(1), 1–19.

Lupinacci, J., & Happel-Parkins, A. (2016a). Ecocritical Foundations: Toward Social Justice and Sustainability. In J. Diem (Ed.), *The Social and Cultural Foundations of Education: A Reader* (pp. 34–56). New York: Cognella.

Lupinacci, J., & Happel-Parkins, A. (2016b). (Un)learning Anthropocentrism: An EcoJustice Education Framework for Teaching to Resist Human-Supremacy in Schools. In S. Rice, & A. Rud (Eds.), *The Educational Significance of Human and Non-Human Animal Interactions: Blurring the Species Line* (pp. 13–30). New York: Palgrave.

Mannion, G., Biesta, G., Priestley, M., & Ross, H. (2011). The Global Dimension in Education and Education for Global Citizenship: Genealogy and Critique. *Globalisation, Societies and Education*, 9(3–4), 443–456. https://doi.org/ 10.1080/14767724.2011.605327.

Martusewicz, R., & Edmundson, J. (2005). Social Foundations as Pedagogies of Responsibility and Eco-Ethical Commitment. In D. W. Butin (Ed.), *Teaching Social Foundations of Education: Contexts, Theories, and Issues* (pp. 71–92). Mahwah: Lawrence Erlbaum Associates.

Martusewicz, R., Edmundson, J., & Lupinacci, J. (2015). *EcoJustice Education: Toward Diverse, Democratic, and Sustainable Communities*, (2nd ed.). New York: Routledge.

McCown, D., Reibel, D., & Micozzi, M. S. (2010). Teaching Mindfulness. *A Practical Guide for Clinicians and Educators*. New York: Springer.

McDonough, K., & Feinberg, W. (2003). Liberalism and the Dilemma of Public Education in Multicultural Societies. In K. McDonough, & W. Feinberg (Eds.), *Citizenship and Education in Liberal-Democratic Societies: Teaching for Cosmopolitan Values and Collective Identities*, pp. 139–145. Oxford: Oxford University Press.

McLaren, P., & Bosio, E. (2022). Revolutionary Critical Pedagogy and Critical Global Citizenship Education: A Conversation with Peter McLaren. *Citizenship Teaching & Learning*, 17(2), 165–181. https://doi.org/ 10.1386/ctl_00089_1.

Mezirow, J. (1996). Contemporary Paradigms of Learning. *Adult Education Quarterly*, 46(3), 158–172. https://doi.org/10.1177/0741713696046 00303.

Mezirow, J. (2000). Learning to Think Like an Adult: Core Concepts of Transformation Theory. In J. Mezirow, & Associates (Eds.), *Learning as*

Transformation: Critical Perspectives on a Theory in Progress (pp. 3–33). San Francisco: Jossey-Bass.

Mezirow, J. (2003). Transformative Learning as Discourse. *Journal of Transformative Education*, *1*(1), 58–63.

Mezirow, J. (2009). Transformative Learning Theory. In J. Mezirow, E. Taylor, & Associates (Eds.), *Transformative Learning in Practice: Insights from Community, Workplace, and Higher Education*, pp. 114–128. San Francisco: Jossey-Bass.

Mignolo, W. (2000a). *Local Histories/Global Designs: Coloniality, Subaltern Knowledges, and Border Thinking*. Princeton: Princeton University Press.

Mignolo, W. (2000b). The many faces of cosmo-polis: Border thinking and critical cosmopolitanism. *Public Culture*, *12*(3) (pp. 721–48).

Mignolo, W. D., & Walsh C. E. (2018). *On Decoloniality: Concepts, Analytics, Praxis*. Duke University Press, Durham (North Carolina, United States).

Miller, D. (2002), Cosmopolitanism: A Critique. *Critical Review of International Social and Political Philosophy*, *5*(3), 80–85.

Noddings, N. (2005). Global Citizenship: Promises and Problems. In N. Noddings (Ed.), *Educating Citizens for Global Awareness* (pp. 1–21). New York: Teachers College Press.

Noddings, N. (2012). The Caring Relation in Teaching. *Oxford Review of Education*, *38*(6), 771–781. https://doi.org/10.1080/03054985.2012.745047.

Noddings, N. (2018). *Philosophy of Education*. Durham: Routledge.

Nussbaum, M. (2002). Education for Citizenship in an Era of Global Connection. *Studies in Philosophy and Education*, *21*(4/5), 289–303. https://doi.org/10.1023/A:1019837105053.

Nussbaum, M. (2005). Liberal Education and Global Community. *Liberal Education*, *90*(1), 42–47.

Osler, A., & Starkey, H. (2005). *Changing Citizenship: Democracy and Inclusion in Education*. Maidenhead: Open University Press.

Oxley, L., & Morris, P. (2013). Global Citizenship: A Typology for Distinguishing Its Multiple Conceptions. *British Journal of Educational Studies*, *61*(3), 301–325. https://doi.org/10.1080/00071005.2013.798393.

Pashby, K. (2011). Cultivating Global Citizens: Planting New Seeds or Pruning the Perennials? Looking for the Citizen-Subject in Global Citizenship Education Theory. *Globalisation Societies and Education*, *9*(3–4), 427–442.

Pashby, K., & Andreotti, V. D. O. (2016). Ethical Internationalisation in Higher Education: Interfaces with International Development and Sustainability. *Environmental Education Research*, *22*(6), 771–787.

Pashby, K., da Costa, M., Stein, S., & Andreotti, V. (2020). A Meta-Review of Typologies of Global Citizenship Education. *Comparative Education, 56* (2), 144–164. https://doi.org/10.1080/03050068.2020.1723352.

Popkewitz, T. S. (2008). *Cosmopolitanism and the Age of School Reform: Science, Education, and Making Society by Making the Child.* New York: Routledge.

Rizvi, F. (2007). Internationalization of Curriculum: A Critical Perspective. In M. Hayden, J. Levy, & J. Thompson (Eds.), *The Sage Handbook of Research in International Education* (pp. 390–403). London: Sage.

Sharma, N. (2018). *Value-Creating Global Citizenship Education: Engaging Gandhi, Makiguchi, and Ikeda as Examples.* New York: Springer.

Sharma, N. (2020). Integrating Asian Perspectives within the UNESCO-led Discourse and Practice of Global Citizenship Education: Taking Gandhi and Ikeda as Examples. In D. Bourn (Ed.), *Bloomsbury Handbook for Global Education and Learning* (pp. 90–102). Bloomsbury Academic, London.

Shaull, R. (2000). Foreword. In P. Freire (Ed.), *Pedagogy of the Oppressed* (pp. 29–34). 30th Anniversary ed. New York: Continuum.

Stein, S. (2015). Mapping Global Citizenship. *Journal of College and Character, 16*(4), 242–252. https://doi.org/10.1080/2194587x.2015.1091361.

Stein, S. (2018). Beyond Higher Education as We Know It: Gesturing towards Decolonial Horizons of Possibility. *Studies in Philosophy and Education,* Springer (pp. 1–19). https://link.springer.com/article/10.1007/s11217-018-9622-7.

Stein, S., & Andreotti, V. (2021). Global Citizenship Otherwise. In E. Bosio (Ed.), *Conversations on Global Citizenship Education* (pp. 13–36). New York: Routledge.

Swanson, D. M., & Gamal, M. (2021). Global Citizenship Education/Learning for Sustainability: Tensions, 'Flaws', and Contradictions as Critical Moments of Possibility and Radical Hope in Educating for Alternative Futures. *Globalisation, Societies and Education, 19*(4), 456–469.

Swanson, D. M., & Pashby, K. (2016). Towards a Critical Global Citizenship? A Comparative Analysis of GC Education Discourses in Scotland and Alberta. *Journal of Research in Curriculum and Instruction, 20*(3), 184–195.

Tarozzi, M., & Inguaggiato, C. (2018). Implementing Global Citizenship Education in EU Primary Schools: The Role of Government Ministries. *International Journal of Development Education and Global Learning, 10* (1), 21–38. https://doi.org/10.18546/IJDEGL.10.1.03.

Tarozzi, M., & Mallon, B. (2019). Educating Teachers towards Global Citizenship: A Comparative Study in Four European Countries. *London Review of Education, 17*(2), 112–125.

Tarozzi, M., & Torres, C. A. (2016). *Global Citizenship Education and the Crises of Multiculturalism: Comparative Perspectives*. London: Bloomsbury.

Torres, C. A., & Bosio, E. (2020a). Global Citizenship Education at the Crossroads: Globalization, Global Commons, Common Good, and Critical Consciousness. *Prospects, 48*, 99–113. https://doi.org/10.1007/s11125-019-09458-w.

Torres, C., & Bosio, E. (2020b). Critical Reflections on the Notion of Global Citizenship Education: A dialogue with Carlos Alberto Torres in relation to higher education in the United States. *Encyclopaedia Journal of Phenomenology and Education, 24*(56), 107–117. https://doi.org/10.6092/issn.1825-8670/10742.

UNESCO. (2015). Global Citizenship Education: Topics and Learning Objectives. https://unesdoc.unesco.org/ark:/48223/pf0000232993.

United Nations. (2020). *Achieving Our Common Humanity: Celebrating Global Cooperation through the United Nations*. United Nations. www.un.org/en/yearbook/achieving-our-common-humanity.

Veugelers, W., & Bosio, E. (2021). Linking Moral and Social-Political Perspectives in Global Citizenship Education: A Conversation with Wiel Veugelers. *Prospects, 53*, 181–194. https://doi.org/10.1007/s11125-021-09576-4.

Webster, R. S. (2023). Confronting and Agonistic: What Democracy Requires of Curricula. *Curric Perspect*. https://doi.org/10.1007/s41297-023-00220-z.

Weintraub, L., Phillips, P. C., Smith, S., et al. (2006). Forum: Eco-tistical art. *Art Journal, 65*(1), 54–81.

Young, M. (2003). Durkheim, Vygotsky and the Curriculum of the Future. *London Review of Education, 1*(2), 100–119.

Young, M. (2008). From Constructivism to Realism in the Sociology of the Curriculum. *Review of Research in Education, 32*(1), 1–28. https://doi.org/10.3102/0091732x07308969.

Zúñiga, X., Naagda, B. R. A., & Sevig, T. D. (2002). Intergroup Dialogues: An Educational Model for Cultivating Engagement across Differences. *Equity and Excellence in Education, 35*(1), 7–17.

Cambridge Elements ≡

Intercultural Communication

Will Baker
University of Southampton

Will Baker is Director of the Centre for Global Englishes and an Associate Professor of Applied Linguistics, University of Southampton. His research interests are Intercultural and Transcultural Communication, English as a Lingua Franca, English medium education, Intercultural education and ELT, and he has published and presented internationally in all these areas. Recent publications include: *Intercultural and Transcultural Awareness in Language Teaching (2022)*, co-author of *Transcultural Communication through Global Englishes (2021)*, co-editor of *The Routledge Handbook of English as a Lingua Franca (2018)*. He is also co-editor of the book series 'Developments in English as Lingua Franca'.

Troy McConachy
University of New South Wales

Troy McConachy is Senior Lecturer in the School of Education at University of New South Wales. His work aims to make interdisciplinary connections between the fields of (language) education and intercultural communication, focusing particularly on the role of metapragmatic awareness in intercultural communication and intercultural learning. He has published articles in journals such as ELT Journal, Language Awareness, Intercultural Education, the Language Learning Journal, Journal of International and Intercultural Communication, Journal of Intercultural Communication Research, and others. His is author of the monograph *Developing Intercultural Perspectives on Language Use: Exploring Pragmatics and Culture in Foreign Language Learning* (Multilingual Matters), and he has co-edited *Teaching and Learning Second Language Pragmatics for Intercultural Understanding* (with Tony Liddicoat), and *Negotiating Intercultural Relations: Insights from Linguistics, Psychology, and Intercultural* Education (with Perry Hinton). He is also Founding Editor and former Editor-in-Chief (2017–2024) of the international journal Intercultural Communication Education (Castledown).

Sonia Morán Panero
University of Southampton

Sonia Morán Panero is a Lecturer in Applied Linguistics at the University of Southampton. Her academic expertise is on the sociolinguistics of the use and learning of English for transcultural communication purposes. Her work has focused particularly on language ideologies around Spanish and English as global languages, English language policies and education in Spanish-speaking settings and English medium instruction on global education. She has published on these areas through international knowledge dissemination platforms such as ELTJ, JELF, *The Routledge Handbook of English as a Lingua Franca* (2018) and the British Council.

About the Series

This series offers a mixture of key texts and innovative research publications from established and emerging scholars which represent the depth and diversity of current intercultural communication research and suggest new directions for the field.

Elements in the Series

Translingual Discrimination
Sender Dovchin

Short-Term Student Exchanges and Intercultural Learning
Gareth Humphreys

Intercultural Communication and Identity
Ron Darvin and Tongle Sun

Ethical Global Citizenship Education
Emiliano Bosio

A full series listing is available at: www.cambridge.org/EIIC

Printed in the United States
by Baker & Taylor Publisher Services